GOLD, DOUBLOONS
AND PIECES OF EIGHT

The Autobiography of

HARRY GOLD

———

GOLD, DOUBLOONS
AND PIECES OF EIGHT

Preface by
John Dankworth

Edited by
Roger Cotterrell

Northway Publications
London

Published by Northway Publications
39 Tytherton Road, London N19 4PZ, UK.

Photo pages design, scanning and digital enhancement; and cover artwork processing: David Cotterrell, Pulse Media.

Cover design: Peter Cattermole. Cartoon of Harry Gold by Trog (reprinted by kind permission of Wally Fawkes). Back cover photo courtesy of Musicians' Union.

The publishers acknowledge with thanks the kind permission of copyright holders to reprint the photographs used in this book. Permissions have been sought in all cases where the identity of copyright holders is known.

A CIP Record for this book is available from the British Library.

ISBN 0 9537040 0 9

First published 2000

Printed and bound in Great Britain by Anthony Rowe Ltd. Chippenham, Wiltshire.

This book is dedicated to the memory
of my dear Margaret (Peggy) Alexander,

to my four sons Morton, Leslie, David and
Andrew,

and to my brother Laurie for his devoted
efforts while with the Pieces of Eight and
afterwards.

Grateful thanks are also extended to the
many friends and colleagues who have
helped along the way.

CONTENTS

PREFACE

The ability to create music is a rare gift, granted by the Controlling Force up there to relatively few of us down here. Amongst our teeming billions on Mother Earth perhaps only one in a thousand (the figures may be even more startling – I am no mathematician) attains any real proficiency in the world of musical self-expression. Of that dwindling band only a handful attain national or international status in their chosen field.

Small wonder. To emerge from this lottery as a successful professional musician – in no matter which of the many styles of music – you will need to stand out in several if not all of a number of categories.

The ability to control and charm an inanimate wood or metal device into producing beautiful sounds is one, but converting this gift into something people will pay for is quite another. And again, the skill to organise and direct a musical group coherently and expertly is a rare one, yet to do it in a way that stands out amongst one's peers is much, much rarer. And yet again, to create or observe the discipline of written notes and harmonies is a special talent, but to convert such inanimate jottings into a rich, living panoply of memorable sounds is something very much more special.

It goes without saying to anyone familiar with Harry Gold's work that this gifted musician's achievements fall into the latter categories of each of the requirements I have listed above – his success in the British musical scene bears quite adequate testimony to that. But to Harry's list of qualities as a musician one other factor must be added – longevity.

I have often said that the greatest thing a jazz musician can do for his career is to die young. Instances abound of great talents being cut off at what should have been the prime of life

– Bix Beiderbecke, Bunny Berigan, Jimmy Blanton, Clifford Brown and countless other lesser-knowns. Heroic figures all, but one sometimes wonders what would have happened had they survived and continued their musical careers. Some would no doubt have gone on to even greater heights; yet others might well have declined in interest and skills and ended their careers in a rather anticlimatic *decrescendo*, soldiering on courageously but perhaps ill-advisedly.

Not so Harry. His musical standards remained constant throughout his long journey in British music, as vibrant and sparkling in the months before his decision to call a halt to his active role as they were when I first encountered and worked alongside the Pieces of Eight in the 1950s. Harry will never be accused by posterity of enhancing his career by departing this world prematurely; that will never be his claim to fame. But his ability to maintain and even further hone his gifts over such an extraordinarily large expanse of musical endeavour is a shining example to succeeding generations of aspiring musicians.

I will always remember Harry's response in accepting a British Jazz Award for services to the music, on the occasion of his ninetieth birthday. I hope I will be forgiven if I get the actual wording a little wrong, but he said in effect: "Thank you very much, but – what nonsense! It is the other way around. It is British jazz that I should be honouring for giving me a wonderful life full of music as well as a happy and successful career."

I am sorry to disagree with that typically modest statement, but those awarding the prize got it right. Thank you so much, Harry, for your great and devoted contribution to our history.

JOHN DANKWORTH
Sonoma, California
August 18th 1999

INTRODUCTION

Harry Gold's vivid, detailed reminiscences of his eight decades as a working musician conjure up lost worlds: London's poverty-stricken East End in the early 1920s; the glamorous high-society life of great dance bands in the inter-war years; dodging bombs in the Blitz; and life on the road with his own jazz band in the post-war decades. His story is populated by royalty, gangsters, fearsome landladies and Irish publicans, but above all by the dozens of jazz and dance band musicians whose talents, eccentricities and often anarchic humour he celebrates. He provides a panorama of the world of popular music in Britain through much of the twentieth century. As he says: have sax, will travel.

Harry's life as a musician was set when as a boy he heard the Original Dixieland Jazz Band at Hammersmith, on their famous visit to Britain in 1919-20 which started the jazz age as far as this country was concerned. As he tells in the following pages, he never forgot that great experience. His own exploits extend from his proving days as a sideman and leader in many bands in the 1920s, through engagements as a star saxophonist and arranger in the 1930s and 1940s with top dance orchestras of the day – most notably, Roy Fox and Oscar Rabin, but also Geraldo, Ambrose and others. Then there were the touring, broadcasting and recording years with his own highly successful Pieces of Eight. After his nominal retirement from full time bandleading, his other career as an arranger, orchestrator and composer continued to flourish.

Harry's activities in music have involved him with most of the legendary names of the British jazz and popular music scene, not to mention the many international stars with whom he has mixed and worked. And he came to know his way around the professional worlds of popular music publishing and orchestration, as well as the broadcasting and recording studios, becoming a household name in popular music in the post-war years.

Composer-arranger, leader, soloist, tireless advocate of that monster of musical plumbing, the bass saxophone (which he turns into an instrument for making swinging, inventive jazz), he is a man of many parts. Widely experienced but far from a jack of all trades, he is very definitely master of the one he knows above all – the business of music, which he loves and which has animated his life.

I heard Harry play on occasions in the 1980s and 1990s, but had no real connection with his life and music before beginning to collaborate with him on this book. The event that led to our meeting was a Labour Party gathering in 1998 at which he and his band provided the music. I was amazed at the verve with which, at 91 years of age, he soloed on bass saxophone, directed the band, led the ensembles, berated the audience when it was slow in getting up to dance, and led everyone in a rousing rendition of the 'Red Flag'. This in itself suggested a political zeal as undiminished as the zeal that drives his music.

Having discovered that he was living just a few streets away from me, I wrote to him to suggest doing an interview. From the late 1960s to the early 1990s I wrote regularly for publications such as Albert McCarthy's excellent *Jazz Monthly*, the Polish journal *Jazz Forum* with its unparallelled coverage of the international jazz world, and most recently Tony Russell's *Jazz FM*. The magazines had all folded. But I had a yearning to dabble again in one way or another in some of this activity, giving something back to the music.

Harry has, of course, been interviewed many times. I thought it might be possible to find a new angle, though a lot of research would be needed given my lack of expertise in the traditional and mainstream jazz styles that he favours. After a while his reply by letter came. It was friendly and helpful. He said he would be happy to accommodate me but would have to postpone the meeting for a while. He was busy writing his autobiography and had promised himself he would finish it that summer. I wrote back that this was excellent news, the autobiography would probably answer all my questions and I would look out for its publication and greatly enjoy reading it.

That seemed to be that. Then after a couple of months another letter arrived. Harry had found a copy of *Jazz Now,* a book which I edited for the Jazz Centre Society in the late 1970s and which contained much material about jazz in Britain. "I think we should meet," said the letter, so we did, at a local pub, on a fine evening in September 1998. He asked me to help him complete his autobiography. He had brought the draft manuscript along to show me. This book is the result of the collaboration we began then.

Harry gave me his manuscript to read and asked me to edit it, adapting it as I thought fit to make it suitable for publication. The only condition was that the writing "must sound like me. It has to be my voice speaking." When we agreed to work together his draft was not quite complete, but he added the few remaining pages in the following months. I put together the text, keeping, wherever possible, not only to what he said but also the way he said it. But I adapted his draft throughout for clarity and, as explained below, over the long period of our discussions much new material has, by various means, been added to it.

I checked facts, wherever possible, from available standard sources and discussed with Harry the relatively few cases where it was hard to reconcile his memories with statements in the reference books. Few dates were given in his draft, but, after consultation with him and with printed reference sources, it proved possible to add a great many to the final text to pinpoint events. That in turn led to some rearrangement of the material to set events in their proper chronological order. On the whole, Harry's memory is amazingly sharp and accurate for a person of any age. The achievement of his memoir is all the more remarkable given that he kept no diary of his career years.

After his draft was completed, we explored together, in many conversations, topics I thought it would be good to say more about, and we cleared up ambiguities or references that seemed obscure, at least to me. In these regular talks over a period of about seven months, Harry supplied a vast amount of detail beyond that contained in his manuscript. I amended and expanded the entire text on the basis of our conversations, broke it up into chapters and added sub-headings. As time went by, he wrote notes about events, anecdotes and stories he thought might be included somewhere. He has approved all parts of the resulting final text.

Apart from putting together the main text in this way, I have added other details separately in more than seventy editorial footnotes placed alongside Harry's narrative. The notes are intended to provide additional background details on musicians and events, where this information seems directly relevant to the story. The books that have been used to gain information are John Chilton's *Who's Who of British Jazz* (Cassell, 1997); Albert McCarthy's *Big Band Jazz* (Barrie & Jenkins, 1974) and his *The Dance Band Era* (November Books, 1971); Phil Hardy and Dave Laing's *Faber Companion to 20th-Century Popular Music* (Faber and Faber, 1990); the *Guinness Who's Who of Fifties Music*, edited by Colin Larkin (Guinness Publishing, 1993); Jim Godbolt's *A History of Jazz in Britain* (two vols, Quartet, 1984 and 1989); Chris Goddard's *Jazz Away From Home* (Paddington Press, 1979); *The New Grove Dictionary of Jazz*, edited by Barry Kernfield (Macmillan, 1988); Ivor Mairants' *My Fifty Fretting Years* (Ashley Mark, 1980); Billy Amstell's *Don't Fuss Mr. Ambrose* (Spellmount, 1986); *The Concise Oxford Companion to the Theatre*, edited by Phyllis Hartnoll and Peter Found (Oxford University Press, 1992); Asa Briggs' *Sound and Vision* (Oxford University

Press, 1979); Kerry Segrave's *Payola in the Music Industry* (McFarland & Co, 1994); and *The London Encyclopedia*, edited by Ben Weinreb and Christopher Hibbert (Macmillan, 1992).

Of these, Chilton's *Who's Who* and McCarthy's *Dance Band Era* have been most important for present purposes. I am deeply indebted to John Chilton's invaluable work, in particular, for much information.

For other matters connected with this publication I should like to acknowledge help especially from Ann Cotterrell, David Cotterrell, Peter Cattermole and Kevin Henriques.

This book results from a collaboration between a musician whose primary musical influences were set by the jazz of the 1920s and 1930s, and a writer/researcher whose love of music started with Brubeck and bebop and gradually extended both forward and backwards chronologically through jazz history. Harry's jazz values were influenced by such as Adrian Rollini and Eddie Miller, mine more by Miles Davis and John Coltrane. That difference doesn't seem to have mattered at all. Certainly, being able to help Harry tell his story has been a unique pleasure and privilege for me.

He writes in the following pages of good and bad times (though mainly he prefers to remember the good ones) and of the exploits of many musicians with whom he has been involved over the years. He conjures up the era of the great dance bands and the glittering venues of a high society life that disappeared with the bombs of the Blitz. He gives many insights into the relationships between jazz and popular music in Britain in the 1920s, 1930s and 1940s. And he suggests something of the dilemmas of musicians trying to make music they found satisfying in and around the contexts of the commercial dance bands. Harry talks about life as an arranger, jazz soloist, bandleader and popular broadcasting musician, and gives the reader a real sense of life on the road as a touring musician.

Not least, he has very important things to say about the politics of the music business and the way it has evolved, the conditions in which musicians have worked and the struggles (in which he was actively involved) to guarantee them a decent recompense for their efforts. Throughout, he tells his story with warm humour and an ear for a good anecdote.

His book celebrates the special magic which jazz and popular music at its best creates. For dancers and listeners, musicians are *magicians* who conjure up atmosphere and mood, transforming rooms that may look ordinary by day into places of musical romance, excitement, fun and pleasure by night. Harry pictures for us the Café de Paris in the 1930s, filled with the velvet sounds of dance music. He lets us imagine numerous venues around the country playing host to his Pieces of Eight on tour, each of these places filled for an evening with the sound of vibrant dixieland. The band might arrive after a long, wearying drive to what could be, after all, just another gig. But for those who had come to hear the music it would be a night out for enjoyment, away from everyday cares. Harry has never forgotten that aspect of music and this is part of the secret of his success.

Here is the story of a man who has spent his long life helping to create magic, giving people memorable experiences of the fun, excitement and romance of music over many decades.

ROGER COTTERRELL

1.

'BEGINNERS PLEASE'

One of my memories from long ago is of the smell of tobacco filling a little shop. My mother Hetty's parents, David and Rebecca Schulman, ran a tobacconist's in the East End of London. Rebecca made cigarettes there by hand. She was quick and skilful. She would pin a piece of thick paper, like parchment, to the table. On it, the tobacco would be rolled out thinly into a pencil shape and pushed into tubes of cigarette paper. Then she would trim off the tobacco sticking out of the ends of the paper with special shears, like elaborate scissors. All this was done at great speed. Meanwhile, David blended the tobaccos, using many different kinds. I remember him in his top hat and his elegant moustache. He knew every trick of the tobacco trade.

They were Romanian. Years before, they had emigrated from Sorroca in Bessarabia (a Romanian province ruled by Russia until the Russian Revolution of 1917). David grew tobacco and traded in it there. Under Russian rule, the trade became a government monopoly, but he was allowed to carry on as long as he looked after the tobacco grown by the chief of police and the local magistrate. The arrangement didn't last. The Schulmans were forced to leave one night in the middle of winter when the Russians seized their farm. They crossed the frozen River Dniestra to escape, carrying their few belongings by hand. Eventually they came to England.

David joined the tobacco trading firm of Richard Lloyd, which sent him to Montreal to help develop a new branch. There he created a blend of tobacco known as 'Sweet as a

Rose'. When he came back to England he opened his tobacconist shop in the East End of London. He sold handmade cigarettes containing his own blend of tobaccos. They were also supplied to various embassies. He died in 1937 aged 74. Rebecca died in 1955 but I never knew her age. She was a very soft, kind and loving woman. She never seemed to get angry with anyone, except maybe occasionally with David. I loved them very much – a feeling that was reciprocated.

The other side of my family came from Germany. My father's father, Louis Gülfuchs, was born in the Black Forest town of Karlsruhe. Louis was a clarinet player, a fat man who towered over me. When I was a small child, he seemed enormous to me. He had a big red beard and, of course, he spoke German.

When he was 22 he married. Since he wanted to avoid military service he changed his name to Goldberg and the couple went to live in Poland. Louis and Hannah had nine children born in Poland. Later the family emigrated to England. Two more children, Sam, my father, and my Aunt Martha were born there. Martha disappeared 'under a cloud' and went to America. I don't know what the 'cloud' was, but her name was never to be mentioned again. I never saw grandmother Hannah. She died after the birth of Martha, no doubt from the strain of too much childbearing. But I knew grandfather Louis who died in 1916 at the age of 84.

Overture

Sam and Hetty, my parents, went to live in Ireland for a time and I was born in Dundrum, County Dublin, on February 26th 1907. Of course, I was Harry Goldberg originally but my father dropped the suffix 'berg' during the First World War because of anti-German feeling. So we became the Gold family. I'm the eldest of six children. My sister Vi (we called her Birdie within the family) was born nearly two years after me. Sid, the next in age, became a drummer who played in night clubs in London's West End and sometimes in touring bands. He was killed in action during the Second World War. Then there was another sister, Bessie. The fifth among the children, my surviving brother, Laurie, is eleven years younger than I am. Like me, he is a saxophonist. He is well known as a musician and has played an important part in my own career, working with me for many years. Another sister Sylvia is the youngest of the children.

I don't remember much about my earliest years in Ireland. I know I was taken every morning to a cow shed and given a warm glass of milk straight from the cow. It seems I was a skinny little runt of a boy who didn't put on any weight. In the light of modern medical knowledge, it's a miracle I'm still around, given that tuberculin testing was unheard of then – but that's what the doctor ordered.

I've always been surrounded by music of one kind or another. When I was a child, radio and television were unknown but there were weekend parties in neighbours' houses with singing, and many of the houses had a piano in the parlour as well as an aspidistra plant in the front window.

Grandfather Louis used to play his clarinet at weddings, though I never heard him play. Sam, my father, told me that he (Sam) broke the instrument and it was never repaired. But, like other families, we had a piano. I can remember my father playing it when I was about three, and I can recollect very clearly his rendering of songs of the day. He sang in a fine tenor voice.

He was a tailor who made everything by hand. He would sit crosslegged on top of a table, underneath a suspended gaslight, sewing away, singing songs like 'Come Into the Garden Maud' and bits of arias from operas. One ditty he sang went like this:

'Life is a kind of apothecary shop / Guess what it isery / A joy and a misery / Sold like a pill with / Sugar on the top / It's a mixture.' I don't know what the origin of that song was. Sometimes he reached so high in a falsetto that his voice sounded like a woman singing. To my childish, uneducated ear it was very beautiful and I was entranced by it.

I suppose you could say this was my first introduction to music. Sam had never been trained as a musician and only played piano by ear. As the Irish would say, 'he was gifted'. My parents remembered that I loved that piano and I regarded it as my own property. During one of our many house moves I watched the furniture being removed with complete indifference until the men started to move the piano. Then I came to life, kicking them and shouting "No! It's my piano."

The Flats

We had moved to England and were living in Leytonstone on the Essex side of London when I was about five. My parents decided then that I should have piano lessons. At the time I was enrolled as a pupil at Davies Lane School, which adjoins Wanstead Flats. The school and the 'Flats' turned out to be a fatal combination. Practising piano scales and playing with my new-found friends on the 'Flats' didn't mix at all well. A tug of war went on between parental discipline, which insisted on piano practice, and the magnetic drawing power of the wide-open spaces, which in winter included a frozen pond on which everyone skated. It ended in victory for the 'Flats'.

My piano teacher was a tyrant who smacked my hands every time I played a wrong note or used a different fingering from the marked one. This made me rebel one day and I stayed away from the weekly lesson. My parents decided the lessons should end and the teacher was given the D.C.M ('Don't

Come Monday'). Strangely enough, after the teacher had been dispensed with, I started to play the piano, picking out tunes with one finger.

One day on the way home from school (I was seven by then), I saw a placard with huge black letters – 'ENGLAND DECLARES WAR ON GERMANY'. The excitement was intense and it seemed that most people were quite delighted with the impending battle for supremacy. At that time, in 1914, we lived at 671 High Road, Leytonstone (there is a garage on the site now). It had a double-fronted shop window in which my father displayed children's clothing which he and my mother made. It seemed that since the declaration of war people were buying more clothes for their children.

One day, a woman came in to buy a little boy's suit of unusual design. I was in the shop and, as my father was in the back room working, my mother was serving. The customer asked if the price could be reduced, so my mother went to the back room to ask if my father would take less. There, in front of my eyes, the woman picked up the little suit and calmly walked out with it. I called my parents but they were too late. She had disappeared.

Instead of my father going into a rage (which he was quite capable of doing) he went to the piano and started to play music I had never heard before. I don't know to this day whether he was just expressing his sadness by composing, or whether the music was well known to him. I still haven't heard anyone else play any of those themes and I've often wondered what would have been the consequence had he been a trained musician.

One night he came into my bedroom to waken me. I could hear a lot of loud bangs and he said, "Come downstairs, there's an air raid." The explosions went on for a considerable time and then suddenly there was silence. We went out to the street to see what was happening. The people who lived over

Janes' drapery store on the other side of the road called to us, "Come over and have a look." In the sky was a huge cigar-shaped airship caught in a blaze of searchlights, one moment seemingly perfectly motionless and the next a blazing inferno. It was the Zeppelin L21 which was shot down by Lieutenant Leefe Robinson of the Royal Flying Corps; one of the celebrated exploits of the air war over London. It was sometime around two o'clock in the morning and, as the flames grew brighter, the cheers got louder and there was much hugging and kissing.

This was early September 1916. It was also the eve of another family move, westward, to the East End of London. My father had received call-up papers for military service. But when he reported to the medical board to be examined he was graded C3 – unfit for active service – because of bad eyesight. He was told that he would have to do civilian work of national importance; in this case, making uniforms for the troops. It was in the East End that most working tailors were to be found and uniform manufacturing required a large workshop to cope with the quantities required.

Chamber Street

After Leytonstone, Chamber Street in the East End, where we next went to live, was a horrid place. The house had no inside toilet or bathroom (previously we had both). I was delegated to cut newspapers into strips for use in the privy in the yard. No-one used toilet paper, at least in the poorer areas. To bathe, we went on Friday nights to the public 'slipper baths' provided by the Council. Inside, the walls were covered with decorative white tiles and there were rows of separate bathroom cubicles with heavy metal doors. Inside each cubicle, the attendant would fill the bath with hot water. After a while you would hear shouts from the cubicles: "More hot in number 9" (or whatever the cubicle number was) or "More cold".

Chamber Street itself was narrow, dirty and close to some railway arches. Under them were the stables that housed the railway's horses and carts. We sheltered in the stables whenever there was an air raid warning. The neighbours got together to organise an air raid warning patrol. My father's large workshop became the meeting place. A card with a letter 'P' was to be placed in the front windows of the patrol members' houses and every night two of the patrol members would be on guard in the street, taking duty in turns. They also had an arrangement with the local police station that patrol members could call in to see if there was an impending air raid.

This was soon found to be unnecessary. A railway signal box overlooked Chamber Street and residents began to notice that when the light in the box was extinguished it meant that enemy aircraft were approaching. Those on patrol duty then had first to knock up the other patrol members, who in turn would wake everyone in the street shouting "Take cover!". At first, most people would go to the stables, taking blankets and food for the night. But the stench of the horse shit was unbearable and in the end we chose to take our chance and stay at home.

Our next door neighbours were naturalised Germans (there were several in the street) and they were nice people. We were friends with them and bore them no ill will. Whenever there was an impending air raid we were invited to their house where we sat and talked together. We sang songs like 'Alle Vogel Sind Schon Da', a song about the birds being here already (which, given that we were waiting for an air raid, expressed a twisted sense of humour).

Apart from the signal box light we had another source of warning. It was the strange action of our neighbours' dog which unaccountably knew there was something amiss. It never failed. The dog would whine and hide itself under their dresser. When that happened our neighbours would call us to say that there was going to be a raid. Sure enough, there was. It was uncanny, but obviously dogs have some sixth sense.

While living in Chamber Street I became a pupil at Berners Street School. I can't find the street now in the London street directory so I can only assume that it either no longer exists or the name has been changed. On my first morning at the school, after an interview with the headmaster, I had to join the form to which I had been assigned and hand the new teacher a certificate containing information provided by my previous school. But the teacher, Mr. Michaels, completely ignored the certificate in my outstretched hand. Instead, he produced a tuning fork, struck it and asked me to sing a scale (do re mi) based on the note sounded by the fork. This was embarrassing to say the least. There I stood in front of a class of staring boys who were expectantly waiting to see what kind of a mess I would make of it. But I managed the scale.

I wasn't let off the hook so easily. Mr. Michaels struck the fork again. From that he took the starting note a tone higher and commanded "Sing!". He was relentless. He struck the fork again and again, each time setting me a higher note until I had reached the peak of my range. The ordeal ended with an instruction to sit at a desk in the front row.

What I didn't know was that Mr. Michaels was the school music teacher and choir master. He was only interested in pupils who could sing in tune, and seated them not according to studious ability, but vocal range; sopranos here, contraltos there and so on. I now believe I owe a lot to his enthusiasm. As conductor of the school choir he was able to instil into the lads a sincere love of music-making together. He did it so well that we were chosen to represent our area in a schoolboys' festival of song at the Royal Albert Hall.

I've always believed in luck. By that I don't mean that some people are born lucky and others not. Neither do I believe that one's life is pre-ordained. If that were so we would never need to do anything to advance ourselves. What I mean by luck is being at the right place at the right time, meeting people who are in a position to help along the way. In this sense, I have been very lucky all through my early years and my professional life. I think it was a bit of luck to have gone to that school where the teacher took music so seriously.

At about this time I had my first experience of dance music. It wasn't the dance music that developed after the introduction of jazz but it was dance music nevertheless. My parents and I were guests at my uncle's wedding reception which took place in a hall in the East End known as Cottage Grove. All the ladies had small programmes with pencils attached. The programmes listed the dances so that partners could be decided in advance and pencilled in against each dance. Among the dances listed were items like the Lancers, Reel, Valse (a quick tempo waltz), Onestep and Turkey Trot.

I don't remember the bandleader's name, but a large board on an easel advertised him as '...the famous dancing violinist'. I wouldn't know how famous he was, if at all, but it seemed that he was trying to introduce the 'new' music of the period while prancing about on the stage in all kinds of steps and contortions. He played foxtrots and other 'modern' dances, totally ignoring the items listed on the ladies' programmes. None of this went down well with the assembled guests. My newly wedded uncle asked him to play a Cossackski, which is a Russian Cossack dance. The bandleader declared rudely that he didn't know it. After a short, excited altercation, my uncle punched Mr. Dancing Violinist on the nose with such force that the blood started to flow freely.

Consternation in the camp! The violinist ran out of the hall and soon returned with a policeman. Eventually my uncle was marched to the police station (on his wedding day of all days) accompanied by the bandleader. But no formal charges were laid and he was allowed to return to the hall. Surprisingly enough, the violinist returned too, to finish the engagement in spite of the earlier fracas.

Apart from the fact that this was my first introduction to live dance music, it was also the first of many fist fights I saw during my professional life and it taught me to be very careful when unable to play requests.

The ODJB

Eventually there was yet another family move, this time to Jubilee Street, also in the East End. There my father had his own tailoring workshop which occupied the top part of the house. I lived there from the end of the First World War until I left home for my real first professional engagement at Rochester Palais. Our house, No 31, doesn't exist any more. Most of the houses around there were destroyed by Hitler's bombers in World War II and replaced by high rise blocks of flats – to my mind, no improvement. The one saving grace is the George pub, which is still standing there just the way it was all those years ago.

Sam, my father, made up clothing for several West End firms and every Saturday morning he had to go to these stores to collect money for the week's work. While he did this, my mother and my sister Vi and I would make our way to the gallery entrance of one of the West End theatres to queue to get front row seats. Sam would join us after collecting the money.

There were many musicals on at the theatres at the time. There was 'The 'Bing Boys' with George Robey at the Alhambra, 'Hullo America' with Fred Astaire and his sister

Adele at the Palace, and 'Chu Chin Chow' with Oscar Asche at His Majesty's Theatre in the Haymarket (now Her Majesty's). What a delight it was to listen to the music coming from the orchestra 'pit', down in front of the stage. All those shows had large orchestras with full wind sections: brass with lots of violins and other members of the string section, even harpists. I saw 'Chu Chin Chow', a musical based on the story of Ali Baba and the forty thieves, four times. Frequently my eyes would wander from the stage to the pit, watching with a secret longing to be there with the musicians.

It was about that time that I encountered one of the most important influences in my musical life. Everyone was talking about an American band called the Original Dixieland Jazz Band which had come to Britain. In it were trumpeter Nick La Rocca, clarinettist Larry Shields, trombonist Emile Christian, pianist J. Russell Robinson and drummer Tony Sbarbaro. Unknown to me at that time they had been performing since the beginning of April 1919 in London at the Hippodrome, the Palladium and elsewhere, to mixed reviews. A year later they were at the Hammersmith Palais and were a sensation. In place of Robinson they were then employing a British pianist, Billy Jones, with whom I played later.

I persuaded my father to take me to hear the ODJB at the Palais and, although I didn't understand what they were doing, the effect was electric. Then and there I resolved to be a musician. To this day that sound of the band has never left me and although I have many of their recordings, the records don't affect me in the same way. I suppose that is the difference between recorded music and live performance.

I left school when I was 14. I had won a place at a grammar school, the Whitechapel Foundation, but I wasn't able to continue because my parents could not afford to keep me there. The school uniform and books had to be paid for and I was needed to help with the family income, working in my father's workshop.

While I was learning the tailoring trade, a new law was passed requiring employers to allow their young employees to have a day away from work to attend what was called 'continuation school'; a system similar to the one that has operated more recently in spheres like printing and architectural studies. I was able to have lessons in mathematics, science, woodwork, metalwork and – wonder of wonders – music.

As an employer of labour my father reacted as many others have done and probably still do. He thought I was wasting my time on 'book learning' when I could be usefully employed in the workshop. I should add that I was not employed on a weekly wage but paid on the basis of production – that is, so much per piece. So I was in a sweatshop situation where I had to work as quickly as possible and as long as possible to make as much money as possible. It meant that while I was on day release, not only was I not earning any money, but the work I should have done was left undone. Some people might applaud that piece work system but, having been on the receiving end of it, I wouldn't and couldn't. I was more determined than ever to become a musician.

Summer was always a very busy time in the tailoring trade. The busy season started with the Easter holidays and ran right through to the autumn. I took advantage of the hours of slogging, sometimes working throughout the night and all next day to make enough money to buy a saxophone. Eventually my post office balance seemed sufficient. My cousin and friend Ben Hornick came with me one Saturday morning to Ebblewhite's musical instrument shop in Aldgate to help choose the saxophone.

Mr. Kimmel

I had the cash in my pocket and I looked for some time at all the instruments in the window – banjos, guitars, clarinets and saxophones of all kinds, shapes and sizes. I hadn't a clue. Fortunately I decided not to buy then but to get advice from Harry Benson, another cousin, who was a cellist playing in an orchestra at Lyons Oxford Street Corner House. He became a 'fixer' years later – a booker of musicians for conductors, etc. – and was my bass player for a while. Harry told me that the flautist in the orchestra at the Corner House was a professor of music who could teach any instrument. I was introduced to him and it turned out that he was Louis Kimmel, a well-known professor at the London College of Music.

Mr. Kimmel made an appointment to meet me at Lewin Brothers' shop in Moor Street, Cambridge Circus, where he tested two or three alto saxes before allowing me to part with my money. I realise now how important that testing was. An instrument not properly in tune can be the downfall of any beginner, who would develop intonation faults difficult to correct. Another example of luck! The sax, which was silver plated, cost me £25.

I studied with Louis Kimmel for five years, first at home and then, on his advice, going to the college to learn clarinet, oboe (which he called 'oyboy'), and keyboard harmony which included imitative counterpoint and orchestration. I suppose that none of that would have happened had I rashly bought the instrument I set out to purchase.

All through my youth we had a wind-up gramophone at home and my father bought records of singers such as Caruso, Galli-Curci, Tetrazzini and Chaliapin. There were also orchestral records but nothing that resembled, even remotely, the music that captivated my imagination at the Hammersmith Palais.

After the 1914-18 War had ended, what we called then the 'wireless' came into popular use. I could never understand why they called it the wireless – there were wires everywhere. My father bought a crystal set (a simple form of radio) with headphones and it was through that medium that I began to hear music vaguely like that of the Original Dixieland Jazz Band. The broadcasts came from the radio station at Savoy Hill whose call sign was 2 LO, and the regular broadcasters were Sidney Firman's London Radio Dance Band, Debroy Somers' Savoy Orpheans and the Savoy Havana Band.

I tried to emulate the sounds I heard via the radio, which didn't go down too well with Louis Kimmel. As was the case with my earlier piano lessons, the exercises the professor set were boring. Long notes, breathing exercises and scales for hours on end were not my idea of playing what I wanted to play. Fortunately for me, Mr. Kimmel had a lot more patience than my piano teacher. He also had the ability to explain carefully why it was necessary to practise in that way. "Don't run before you can walk," he said. So I practised long notes every day until I could hold a note at a whisper for an unbelievably long time. Soon I found that he was giving me more and more of his valuable time at no extra charge. He was the kind of person who would give everything he'd got if he was interested in a student.

One day he showed me a piece of music he had transcribed from Saint-Saëns' composition 'The Swan'. It was intended as a sight reading test. It is a slow piece so it wasn't difficult for me and I played it straight off without a mistake, feeling proud of myself. But pride goeth before a fall. The balloon was pricked in a second. "There is more to music than notes," he declared. "There is no expression, no feeling in your playing." He was very painstaking and took me through the piece over and over again, explaining every detail. It was a bit like one of the present day master classes and it went on until he was completely satisfied that I knew what he was aiming for.

Some time later he asked if I could afford to buy a soprano saxophone. "I would like to organise a saxophone quartet made up of my best students, which will provide some pleasurable practice," he explained. He wanted to arrange some 'straight' compositions for a quartet so that we could get some experience playing as a unit rather than as soloists. I was still working as a tailor then, and earning reasonably good money, so I said I would buy the soprano. By then I knew how to test instruments for myself, so I went off to Lewin Brothers again to make the new purchase.

One gorgeous piece he had arranged was 'Praeludium', a prelude and orchestral work by Armas Järnefelt. The instrumentation was soprano, alto, tenor and baritone saxophones and I found it exhilarating. So it diverted me away from trying to play music like the Original Dixieland Jazz Band. Of course, my earlier musical background must have had some influence on my feelings for that side of musical expression.

The quartet practised regularly, continually increasing our repertoire, and eventually we entered a 'do-as-you-please' competition at the Mile End Empire theatre. We won our heat and came second in the Saturday night final. What excitement and encouragement that was. But it was still a very far cry from the ODJB.

Just about that time our household suffered a double tragedy. My brother Laurie who was a young child then, had an eye pierced by a toy bow and arrow. Soon afterwards my middle sister, Bessie, was killed, having been run over by a lorry on her way home from school. She was coming home for dinner and was wearing a Red Riding Hood mackintosh. The bottom of it swung out in the wind and got caught in the rear nearside wheel of the lorry. She died instantly. It became impossible to practise for a long time after those events, but the professor was very understanding and kept my place open until I was able to resume my studies.

"It Sounds Like a Band!"

Eventually Mr. Kimmel started to let me play from printed band parts. That was when I began to see the value of the endless practising. Everything fell into place. Soon afterwards, I saw an advertisement in a local newspaper: 'Wanted, a saxophone player willing to rehearse. Write to Joe Loss, Grey Eagle Street, E.1.' Yes, it was THE Joe Loss, who later became one of the most famous dance bandleaders in Britain.[1] I wrote to him and he replied asking me to call at his house where we would rehearse.

Here, once again, was luck coming in to help. I wasn't to know that Joe would one day become famous and be in a position to help me. Many years after my first meeting with him he was working at the Hammersmith Palais. I was told that the relief band at the Palais was leaving so I phoned Joe to ask if this was true. He said it was and would I be interested? Needless to say, I was, and I got the job with my band, the Pieces of Eight. But I'm jumping ahead...

On arriving at Joe's house for the first rehearsal I found waiting for me a drummer (Harry Marco), a lady pianist whose name I don't remember, and Joe, violin in hand. Also present was another man whom I later found out was a professional drummer known in the business as Ginger Conn.

---

[1] Joe Loss, born in 1909, had studied violin at Trinity College of Music and the London School of Music. He turned professional in 1926 and led highly successful dance and variety orchestras for nearly six decades, broadcasting, recording (including pop hits in the 1960s) and touring extensively (Ed.).

He was a friend of Joe's and I suppose he was there to audition the newcomer.

The first shock was that the pianist could only play by ear and only on the black notes. She couldn't play the written keys. Shock number two was that both Joe and I had to read the music from piano song copies placed on the piano, leaving little elbow room for either of us. Shock number three was that as the pianist was not playing in the same key as the written piano parts, both Joe and I had to change the written notes to conform to the pitch that the pianist was playing – a worse problem for me than for Joe. Although we both had to transpose the written notes, I had to do a double transposition because my alto sax was pitched in the key of E Flat whilst the violin is a concert pitched instrument, as is the piano. I had to transpose not only for the pitch of my instrument, but also for the key in which the piano part was written but not being played. Confusing isn't it? I hope you're still reading! Anyway, the experience was useful. I quickly became adept at transposing anything at sight, and the skill has served me in good stead all through my professional life.

By this time I was beginning to make sounds vaguely like those I had been hearing on the 'wireless'. During that audition with Joe Loss in Grey Eagle Street, Ginger Conn went out to the street to hear what the music sounded like from afar. Distance lends enchantment. He came back full of enthusiasm, saying "Hey Joe, it sounds like a real band!" I suppose the addition of the saxophone tone changed the character. We started to get engagements at house parties, mostly for experience and sometimes for a few shillings. Then came an engagement at Bloom's new kosher restaurant in the Whitechapel Road on its opening night. We got half a crown (12½p) and a salt beef supper. Now we were on our way! Many years later I met Ginger Conn in Archer Street (the musicians' 'labour exchange') and we had a good laugh about that audition. (More about Archer Street later.)

Eventually I had to say to Joe that I couldn't carry on playing that way. I wasn't getting any reading practice and I couldn't see any future in it for me. He understood and wished me luck. But some months later he called me and said, "I've found a new pianist who can read music. Are you interested?" Of course I was. It meant getting together with a band that could play from music and a step in the right direction. The pianist's name was Bert Pearlstone and he eventually married my sister Vi (It didn't work out and they parted company). Bert was a good player, up to our standard, and we decided to go after gigs, having chosen the unbelievable name 'The Magnetic Dance Band'. We played quite a few gigs around the East End. On one occasion we played in the same hall as the Ultra Five band. Their pianist was Jimmy Phillips who later became a well known publisher and the head of Peter Maurice Music Company, KPM and later EMI Music Publishing.

One disastrous event for the band was at a hall in Commercial Road called the Grand Palais. We had decided that it might be profitable to hire the hall and organise a public dance and take all the profit. Ha, ha, ha! Discussing the matter with friends, it became obvious that we would need to sell tickets in advance. So we formed a committee from among the friends with each allotted a job. We printed posters and arranged to have someone in the box office selling tickets on the night of the dance. Advance ticket sales were good and on the night the hall was packed. At two shillings and sixpence (12½ pence) per person we should have made £100 after expenses. In fact, we lost £20. Obviously, many people had got in via the exit doors, undoubtedly let in by friends already inside. We hadn't thought about having stewards to watch the exits.

2.

THE METRONOMES, VIC FILMER AND THE FAMOUS FIVE

My first professional job (around 1921) was with a stage band. The bandleader's name was Teddy Morris and the job lasted just two weeks. The vocalist was Ben Levin who later changed his name to become famous as the comedian/singer Izzy Bonn. The first week was a try-out at the Poplar Hippodrome at half-pay. The full weekly money for the job was four pounds and ten shillings but because it was a try-out we were only to get half. The following week was to be at Bedford and was also supposed to be a try-out, also for half-pay. I felt we were being taken for a ride so I left.

Around that time I first worked regularly with Ivor Mairants.[1] I needed to play with a band and immediately contacted Bert Pearlstone and Ivor whom I had met while we were both playing gigs in other bands. Louis Kimmel introduced us to a violinist, Reg Smith, and Bert introduced an alto player named Harry Atkins. Harry, it was reputed, played 'dirt' – the name then for jazz extemporisation. The drummer was Harry Marco from the Magnetic Band. We decided to call ourselves the Florentine Dance Band – about as Florentine as Cleethorpes! The line-up was two alto saxes, piano, violin, drums, and Ivor on guitar and banjo.

---

[1] Ivor Mairants, born in Poland in 1908, had lived in London since 1914 and bought his first banjo at the age of fifteen. He later worked alongside Harry in several bands before both of them joined Roy Fox's orchestra in 1932 (Ed.).

We entered a dance band contest, won the local heat and came second in the final. I was called to play a solo because the judges could not decide who should get the sax prize. I didn't get it. I don't remember who did, except that he was a well known, part-time player.

Archer Street

I was ambitious. I wanted to improve my playing and I felt I needed to know more about music as a business. Harry Atkins' brother Tommy played in a nightclub beside Don Barrigo, a fine saxophone player who was said to have come from South Africa. If so, he must have left that country soon after the First World War because I remember him playing in London when I was fourteen.[2] He lived in the East End, close to Hanbury Street. Harry Atkins told me that Don held free classes every Sunday morning and anyone who was interested would be welcome. So Harry and I went along together to see the great Don Barrigo. He gave us a great deal of information about the music business, including advice that we should go to Archer Street, the place where professional musicians regularly gathered to hire and be hired for bands. He suggested that we should try to meet people in the profession there, and by going frequently we would get known, at least as available for work.

I might mention here, in passing, that I worked with Don Barrigo some years later in a stage band organised by a wealthy young man who had acquired the right to use the famous band title 'Savoy Orpheans' and several of the

---

[2] Chilton's *Who's Who* states that Barrigo was born in London and worked there and in Germany, Denmark and France in the 1920s. He was in Lew Stone's orchestra for six years from 1935 and, after playing with other bands, returned to Stone during 1946 before emigrating to South Africa where he led his own bands, opened a physiotherapy clinic and worked as an actor (Ed.).

Orpheans' original orchestrations[3]. Don helped me then, too. It was a haphazardly organised band that was losing money. Don and I, with Ivor Mairants and the trumpeter Les Lambert, did some dates with it. When it looked as though we were not going to get paid, it was Don who put pressure – to understate the matter somewhat – on the leader to get us our money.

Anyway, I took Don's advice. I went to Archer Street and patiently stood outside the barber shop which faced the Orchestral Association building, making conversation with other young musicians eager to become professionally known. We all stayed on the barber shop side of the street, staring across to the Orchestral Association side where well-known and even famous players stood and cracked jokes while possibly offering each other gigs or information about resident employment with bands. There was a 'cagey' method of telling a musician how much a gig was worth when other people were around, by saying loudly for all to hear "Can you do a gig tomorrow night at the Ritz? It's worth a fiver", and at the same time placing two or maybe three fingers across the lapel of a jacket, which indicated the real fee – two or three pounds.

I once wrote a short story called 'The Other Side of the Street' in which a budding young musician stood precisely where I stood in Archer Street, doing what all the other young, unknown musicians were doing, waiting. Eventually he got a job in a touring band. Thanks to that opportunity he became well known and earned the right to stand with the musicians on the pavement on the Orchestral Association side of the street. He toured for many years and finally left the band. Returning to Archer Street he discovered that new musicians had arrived on the scene. They were the ones standing on the Orchestral Association pavement now and he didn't know a soul. Finally,

---

[3] The Savoy Orpheans, resident at the Savoy Hotel in the Strand, were one of many British dance bands in the 1920s strongly influenced by the style of Paul Whiteman's orchestra which visited London in 1923 (Ed.).

he gradually went over to the other side of the street. That was nearly the story of my life after I left Oscar Rabin's orchestra in 1942, and it taught me how valuable it is to maintain contacts at all times.

During my visits to Archer Street I came across an advert – 'Musicians wanted' – in an entertainments periodical, *The Era*, which was a theatrical paper similar to *The Stage*. Auditions were to be held in a room in Great Newport Street near Leicester Square. I committed the unpardonable sin of arriving late. I heard a band playing and hesitated to open the door, partly embarrassed for being late and partly because it seemed to me that the 'chair' would be already fixed. The band was playing, after all, and it sounded good to me. As matters turned out, the job had indeed been arranged. But I opened the large, stable-like door and poked my head through the opening, to be greeted with laughter when the band stopped playing. I had my alto in one hand, soprano in the other and clarinet under my arm.

I must have presented a strange appearance as I had not yet grown to my present height of five feet two inches. I was also a skinny little runt wearing a bowler hat a size too large which rested on my ears. The bandleader (whose name I don't remember) asked what I wanted. I replied, "I'm sorry I'm late; I've come for the audition." Surprisingly, he allowed me to play and I got the job. I learned later that each sax player they had auditioned was worse than the one before. When I appeared it had seemed like the last straw after a bunch of disappointing performances. They had already decided on the man playing when I arrived, but I think the bandleader felt sorry for me.

We were due to start at Rochester Palais a week before Christmas Eve 1923. What I didn't know was that the job was only for two weeks, ending on New Year's Day. I found this out during the second week and was frantic with worry because I had given up my day job. But the lady of good fortune smiled once more. Dennis Powell, the banjo player, who had given me the information, said "Don't worry, I'm starting at the Lewisham Dance Lounge next Monday and the band there needs a sax player. Are you interested?" I thought: "He's got to be joking – am I interested?" – I was over the moon. From then on I never looked back because it was the beginning of my lengthy professional career.

Winners!

Dennis told me to be at the Lounge at 11.00 a.m. for a rehearsal before the afternoon tea dance session. Remembering what happened at my first audition, I resolved to be on time. I did a spot of practice before leaving home in Jubilee Street. Then I made the ten minutes walk to Whitechapel underground station, travelled by underground under the Thames to Shadwell, changed for New Cross and got a train to Lewisham junction. From there it was a short walk to the Lounge.

I had worked out just how long the journey would take and, to avoid being late, had packed my alto quickly and left Jubilee Street early. When I arrived at the hall, someone from the bandstand called out, "Where's your mouthpiece?". I didn't know what he meant and thought he was just being rude. But in my hurry to pack my instrument I had left the mouthpiece on the table at home. My father had phoned to say he was bringing it.

After the initial introduction by Dennis over a cup of tea, I learned that the band was to be known as Drayson Marsh's London Band. The job was Drayson's originally but he had moved to Sandown on the Isle of Wight. He was playing in a hotel there with his original band. Our personnel was Francis Watson (trumpet), Harold Watson (piano), Dennis Powell (banjo and tenor guitar), Phil Cork (leader, drums and violin) and myself on alto and soprano saxes and clarinet.

My mouthpiece arrived and we began to rehearse. We played from commercial printed parts and also tried some extemporisation. I was pleasantly surprised by the quality of musicianship. They were the best I had played with so far. I was still studying music composition at the college then and I suggested that I should write some special arrangements for the band. I thought it would be good practice for me. So the following Monday I brought my first arrangement to rehearsal. The difference between playing from printed arrangements and from a specially written one was obvious immediately and that encouraged me to keep writing for the band.

We were a co-operative. We all got the same money – six pounds ten shillings (£6.50) a week for six afternoons and six evenings. It was quite good money for those days if you compared it with a bus driver's two pounds ten shillings a week.

After about three months at the Lounge we entered a dance band contest organised for professional bands by *The Era*. The rules required each band to play three pieces, one of which should be a waltz. Two pieces were set by the judges (so all bands had to play those) and the third would be a piece of the band's own choice. I wrote the arrangements for all three. We won both the local heat and the semi-final which was held at the New Cross Palais.

Inside the Palais were stands of various firms exhibiting musical instruments. One of the firms was Lewin Brothers from whom I had bought my first instruments. I went to look at their display and saw a lovely gold plated alto which took my fancy. I was asked to try it during our performance, which I gladly did. When the results of the semi-final were announced I was told I could keep it on a straight swap.

Instrument dealers in those days did that for advertising purposes.

Phil Cork, our leader, could see that the band was going places. By then he had changed the name to the Metronomes. The *Melody Maker* reported that "The winning band at New Cross was the Metronomes. It is only a five-piece band but the arrangements made it sound much larger." My name wasn't mentioned as the arranger, but I was more than delighted.

The finals were to be held at the newly opened Astoria Dance Salon in Charing Cross Road. The period preparing for them was an anxious one for us youngsters, knowing that we were going to be heard in the number one venue in the West End of London. More so for me because I was much younger and the others were more experienced. Once again there were two set pieces (different from those for the semi-final) and one piece of our choice. So, once again, special arrangements were the order of the day and we rehearsed them until we knew them backwards.

Just before the final and on the way to the Lewisham Dance Lounge I fell down a whole flight of steps at Shadwell station and fractured my ankle. I arrived at Lewisham in great pain. My ankle had swollen enormously so the manageress got me to remove my shoe and sock to put cold compresses to the swelling until we were ready to start the afternoon session. I couldn't get my shoe back on so I had to play with one shoe, and a sock on the other foot.

On the day of the final I couldn't walk and had to be carried on to the stand at the Astoria by two attendants. Among the judges were Debroy Somers (conductor of the Savoy Orpheans) and the bandleader and music publisher Herman Darewski who, it was discovered later, had a financial interest in a ladies' band which was one of the contestants.

Before the winner was announced we were asked to play another session against the ladies' band. There was a long wait after that. Then finally came the result: Metronomes first place; the ladies' band second! There had been a lengthy argument among the judges. Darewski wanted the ladies' band to have first place but the other judges plumped for us. We had won in the face of strong opposition from much larger bands and it became clear to me that the arrangements had been a great advantage. A final reward for winning was that we were offered the job of relief band at the Astoria to the then resident band, Howard Baker. Needless to say, we accepted.

The Astoria and the Isle of Wight

After a while, Howard Baker told us that he and his band were leaving the Astoria, and a new band was coming from Southport Palais to replace his. It turned out to be Billy Cotton, who became famous on the radio as 'Mr. Wakey, Wakey'.[4] Billy was the drummer and entertainer. At every session his band put on a floor show which included an apache dance in which Billy did the throwing-about routine while one of the saxophone players dressed up as a female to take the punishment. It was sensational! Apart from that, the band was excellent (most of the members were Scots) and Clem Bernard, the pianist, was also the arranger. I used to practise my writing studies (figured bass, etc.) on the balcony between the afternoon and evening sessions, and Clem would come over to see what I was doing and give me free advice. He was a really nice guy.

---

[4] Billy Cotton, musician and keen sportsman, played drums in various bands, and football for Brentford and Wimbledon, before forming his own band in 1924 to play at the Wembley Exhibition. By the 1930s he was well established as a touring, broadcasting and recording dance band leader. His very popular 'band show' on radio, and – from 1957 – television, mixed comedy and big band music (Ed.).

Many years later, Billy was able to give me some deputising work in his band – on one occasion it was when his lead player was somewhat 'under the weather' just before a broadcast! It only shows how being in the right place at the right time can be lucky. I'm not saying that ability has nothing to do with it. But that other thing – knowing someone who knows someone – does help.

While we were working at the Astoria, Dennis Powell suggested that maybe his father could be the band's manager. He was a pawnbroker in south London and a good businessman so, after discussing it, we agreed to pay him ten per cent of what we received on all engagements. Not long after we had signed agreements with Mr. Powell senior, we were told by him that we would be leaving the Astoria to go into the Prince's Theatre (now the Shaftesbury) to play in the pit for a non-musical show called 'Compromising Daphne', which was a farce. I've never been certain whether or not we had been given notice by the Astoria or whether our new manager gave them notice in order to start collecting his ten per cent.

All we had to do in the show was play a tune for the overture, play during two intervals, and do a play-out and the national anthem at the end. The producer had a great idea – a complete innovation. He had the pit dressed in the style of a drawing room complete with carpet and standard lamps. It had never been done before.

We played tunes that lent themselves to jazz improvisation and in one of them, 'Blue Skies', I sang through a megaphone – there were no microphones at the time. On opening night we were told to be on our toes: the critics would be in and they could make or break us. The following day an article by Hannen Swaffer in the *Daily Herald* pulled the show to pieces. One sentence in it read: "I wish they would stop that dreadful blaring through a megaphone." I suppose you can't please all of the people all of the time.

The show closed soon after an accident occurred. At the time we considered it serious but later thought it funny. In every theatre performance the safety curtain had to be lowered once during the evening. But on the fateful evening at the Prince's Theatre, the person who was supposed to pull the safety curtain lever pulled a different lever by mistake. It was the one that operated the sprinkler system. The musicians in the pit ran for dear life under the stage with whatever instruments we could grab, whilst the audience in the first couple of rows of the stalls got a thoroughly good wetting!

We weren't out of work for long. Our manager got us a job for a season playing in a dance hall on the pier at Shanklin on the Isle of Wight. We played for morning coffee and afternoon tea and did a normal dance session in the evening. That was from May until the end of September 1926. Afterwards there was a winter season in Southampton at the Barova Restaurant in Tyrell and Green's store in the Above Bar area. Again we played for coffee and afternoon tea but the evenings were free. That meant that we could also play for dinner dances in the South Western Hotel. But we weren't getting much more money than when we were playing at the Lewisham Dance Lounge. We had had a slight increase when we moved to the theatre – seven pounds instead of six pounds six shillings (£6.30p). That's what we were paid at Shanklin and Southampton. Of course, when we played at the South Western Hotel we got an extra two pounds for each evening gig, which wasn't bad.

The band was rebooked to play Shanklin for two more seasons, with one in between at the Barova Restaurant. Before we went back to Shanklin we decided that we should have a band uniform suitable for a seaside resort. Up to then, we had worn dinner suits. We agreed that the ideal uniform would be light grey flannel double-breasted jackets and 'Oxford bags' (trousers with twenty six inch bottoms and three inch turn up cuffs), which had become fashionable. My father, being a tailor, was given the order to make them ('keep it in the family'!). But they looked odd on me. I have small feet – size 6 – and so, when I wore my Oxford bags, my shoes could not be seen. Wearing the trousers I looked as though I was gliding along instead of walking.

Summer Days

It was a wonderful time for us in the island every summer. It seemed as though the sun always shone. It was like being paid to be on holiday. Our coffee session in the morning started at eleven o'clock and lasted an hour. The afternoon tea dance lasted two hours, from three o'clock until five. Between those two sessions we spent our time on the beach swimming or kicking a ball about. My mother was worried about me as I'd never been away from home on my own before. She thought I would not get enough to eat, so she sent food parcels which arrived every Friday. They contained a huge volume of goodies, far too much for one person, so the five of us banqueted for two days each weekend.

Apart from the pleasure of the sun and the weekly feast, I realised that I was in an entirely different situation both physically and socially. Figuratively speaking, the umbilical cord had finally been severed. The other members of the band were all much older than I was. They were beer drinkers who dated girls who came into the hall to dance. Of course, I tagged along.

The only girls I had known had been those who came into our Jubilee Street home as friends of my sister Vi or as neighbours' daughters. My parents had kept a tight rein on me and my brothers and sisters. I had also become engaged to my first wife Annie. I had met her because she worked as a buttonhole hand in my father's workshop. But now that I was away from parental control I was seeing other girls who were also away from their families. Overcoming my inhibitions, I too began to 'chat up' girls who came into the hall. It never led to more than a kiss and a cuddle as I was too nervous to enter into any other relationship.

The girls on holiday always wanted to have their photographs taken with the chaps whom they had befriended and always with arms around. Copies were displayed at a kiosk on the promenade with the intention of selling them to the holiday makers.

During our second season at Shanklin, Ivor Mairants and his then fiancée Lily arrived for a holiday, renewing our earlier acquaintance and with both of us totally unaware that we would be working together in a famous band for a considerable period some years later. One day, Ivor said to me almost accusingly, "Harry, there's a photograph of you at the kiosk up the road with your arm around a girl." Panic immediately set in because Annie was arriving that same week. Although the girl in the photograph had already left the island, I knew that it was vital to get the photo removed out of sight. Not only did I buy the copy Ivor saw but also some others that had been printed, as well as the negative. Money well spent I suppose.

The Shanklin-Southampton routine continued until the end of the final (third) summer season, giving the band immeasurable experience, playing light music in the restaurant, dance music in the hotel and, in Shanklin, some jazz. While in Southampton in 1927 for the second winter season and at the tender age of twenty, I married Annie, which meant concentrating on earning more money. It raised thoughts of leaving the band, which did happen at the end of the last summer season.

Also while we were in Southampton, I became friendly with two local sax players who were working in a cafe opposite Tyrell and Green's store. One was Hughie Tripp who later became a member of Roy Fox's band alongside me, and the other was Alfie Morgan who became secretary of the Musicians' Social and Benevolent Council (MSBC).

A momentous event for us young musicians was the visit to Southampton's variety theatre by Jack Hylton's band.[5] We booked seats for the second house on the Monday night and I suggested that we should try to get to meet Hylton between the first and second houses. We were unsure how to go about it, but we finally decided to go to the stage door early and before the first house had ended. We handed our band's business card to the stagedoor keeper with a request to send the card in to Jack Hylton. To our delight, we gained admittance to his presence. He was very kind, and spoke to us about the then current trend for band shows, stressing that we needed to be entertainers as well as musicians. Finally, he asked if we wanted to see the show. We told him we already had seats. Had we known we would have got in for nothing. I thought that Hylton's making himself so accessible was an act of friendly encouragement. I was unaware that the big names I was to meet as the years rolled by were all like that.

During the second season on the Isle of Wight, the other members of the band decided that because of my arranging ability I should lead. That enabled me to get to know the various music publishers who supplied us with printed band

---

[5] Hylton had been leading a dance band since 1921, when he was 29, and he became a phenomenal popular success in the 1920s and 1930s, through records, broadcasts and non-stop touring in Europe presenting a mix of light classics, popular hits, novelty numbers and speciality acts. In the mid-1920s he was often called the English Paul Whiteman but his records of sweet dance music were supplemented with some jazzier material from his recording groups (Ed.).

parts and song copies without charge. That saved us a lot of money and kept us up to date with the latest publications. Of course, it was good publicity for them to have us playing their music.

Most of the publishers had premises in Denmark Street (known as 'Tin Pan Alley'). From time to time I visited these businesses and got to know the managers of them personally. One was Jimmy Phillips. As I mentioned earlier, I had already met him when he was the pianist with a band called the Ultra Five. When he became manager of the Lawrence Wright Music Company I was able to renew the acquaintance. Another person in music publishing was George Seymour, late managing director of Campbell and Connolly. He had been a page boy at the Astoria and he introduced me to Leslie Holmes who was a song plugger (a person who tries to persuade artistes to play or sing the publisher's material). Leslie Holmes formed a partnership with Leslie Sarony as the Two Leslies. Another Les, Les Osborne was a song plugger for Campbell and Connolly. He became a great friend of mine and years later joined me in writing songs when we both worked for EMI. Les, incidentally, was the co-writer of the signature tune of the 'East Enders' TV soap opera.

Once again, because of that lucky change, I was able more and more to meet people who would be able to help me professionally. At the end of the third summer season I was told that our manager had booked the band to go to India. I needed a stay in India like I needed a hole in the head and regretfully we parted company. Having recently become a married man, I thought that I needed to set up a *pied-à-terre*, and going to India would leave us completely dependent on 'digs' (lodgings). I also felt that I should get experience in other directions. Although, when I left the Metronomes at the end of the summer of 1928, I hadn't a job to go to, I was confident that sooner or later one would turn up.

"Why So Nervous?"

While I had been away from London I had been a subscriber to the *Melody Maker* magazine. I subscribed so as to ensure that I regularly received copies by post at the pier-head every Wednesday morning before the paper appeared in the shops. That way I would see the advertisements at the earliest possible time. About three weeks before the Shanklin job ended, I saw an advert requesting applications from alto sax players who could read music and extemporise, for a West London job. I immediately sent a telegram to the advertiser to say that I was able to meet the requirements and would be free at the end of September. Two days later I received a letter asking me to give an audition in a club in Great Newport Street (near Leicester Square). There was a proviso. I would need to know from memory a list of about one hundred tunes, mostly from shows. I didn't know any of them, so I contacted my publisher friends who sent the required copies by return. At the same time I wrote to the advertiser, who had by then revealed his identity as Vic Filmer senior. I told him that I knew all of the tunes. Vic Filmer was a very well known pianist, songwriter and arranger.[6] He had a bass playing son, also named Vic. Hence the 'senior'.

I was elated that I had received a reply so soon but the elation soon changed to bitter disappointment. A week before I left Shanklin a letter arrived to tell me that Vic Filmer had engaged Jack Clapper to play at the Melton Club, Kingsley Street (off Regent Street). The news was verified by a notice in the *Melody Maker*. Jack Clapper and his brother Lionel were very well known West End saxophone players, so I was certain that I had lost the job. But the following day I received a telegram

---

[6] Filmer had worked for Luigi Fortoni's Italian Orchestra from 1920 to 1926. When he formed his own band in 1929, at the age of 32, he was also acting as musical director for Pathétone film company (Ed.).

asking me to go to Great Newport Street after all. I suspect that the money on offer wasn't good enough for Clapper.

I arrived at the appointed time and place and was met by Filmer, who had arranged for me to sit in with a big band that was rehearsing there. There were three saxes, three brass and four rhythm. It was something completely new for me and to say I was nervous would be the understatement of the year. I played through a couple of arrangements as a test of my reading ability. Then I was asked to ad lib on alto, baritone and clarinet in turn. By that time my nerves had got the better of me and I was sure I had failed.

After the audition ended Vic came over and said, "Come and have a cup of tea," taking me through back streets of Soho that I never knew existed. On the way to the cafe he asked, "Why are you so nervous?" I told him, "It was an entirely new situation for me, never having played in a sax section in a big band." Over tea he said, "The money is eight pounds a week for six nights, the place is the Melton Club in Kingsley Street, you start Monday at 11.00 p.m. and you finish when the last customer has gone. Then we will have breakfast!" That often turned out to be 6.00 or 7.00 a.m. So it was a real all-night club. We always got a good breakfast and, for those days, eight pounds a week was very good money. We also got tips for playing requests, which were shared between the members of the band equally.

One night an American customer from the 'Deep South' asked the musicians in the band, "Do you know the rebel cry?" We said "No". He let out a piercing scream and said, "That's it! Whenever you hear me do that, I want you to play 'Dixie' OK?" Then he made a bee-line for the bar. We carried on playing for the crowd and then suddenly from the bar came this loud "YAHOO!". Vic Filmer, who never closed an eye to the opportunity to make a bit on the side, stopped the band dead in the middle of a chorus and went straight in to 'Dixie'.

The American came over and put one of those wonderful, crinkly, white five pound notes into the bell of my saxophone. I immediately handed the note to Vic, while our friendly philanthropist wended his way back to the bar. This happened so frequently that our transatlantic customer ran out of English money and, in the end, we were getting dollars. That morning at breakfast we had the share-out and each of us went home with £30. What a night!

While we were at the Melton Club, I had the opportunity to hear Fred Elizalde's band at the Savoy Hotel.[7] My side-kick on tenor sax in the Filmer band, George Pallat, had suggested we should try to get into the hotel through the kitchens, where we had a friend. We stood behind a large screen to hear Elizalde. His band included the American saxophonists Adrian Rollini and Bobby Davis, trumpeter Chelsea Quealey, and three young English musicians, George Hurley who played excellent jazz violin, and Harry Hayes and Rex Owen on saxes. Little did I know that later I should be working with George in Richard Sudhalter's band, Rex in Roy Fox's band, and Harry with Geraldo.

It was wonderful to hear Adrian Rollini in person. I had been listening to his bass saxophone playing on records and he was the greatest influence on my taking up that instrument and on shaping my style on it. I think of him as a genius. Seeing and hearing him with Elizalde was a very special experience. At that time I heard that he was selling one of his bass saxes which he used for gigs away from the hotel. It had fallen off

---

[7] Pianist-composer Federico ('Fred') Elizalde, born in the Philippines, had arrived in Britain in 1926. He had been leading a band at the Savoy (somewhat controversially because of his reluctance to compromise musically with the wishes of the dancers) since the beginning of 1928. The orchestra, which contained several excellent jazz musicians of the period including imported American stars, disbanded at the end of 1929 and in the 1930s Elizalde was best known as a conductor of symphony orchestras (Ed.).

the top of a car and been badly damaged. I bought it from Rollini for a 'song' and spent a lot of money to put it in playing condition. It was the first bass sax I had ever played. Many years later, to my utter grief, it was stolen. It came back utterly destroyed.

At around the same time, Ted 'Is everybody happy?' Lewis and his band were playing at the Kit Kat restaurant in the Haymarket. Among the personnel were saxophonist Jimmy Dorsey, cornetist Muggsy Spanier and trombonist George Brunies.[8] Dorsey, Brunies and one or two others used to come into the Melton Club after their gig and one night Dorsey came over to me and asked, "Do you mind if I sit in and play your alto?" Needless to say, all of us in the band were delighted and in my excitement I completely forgot the golden rule about not letting other musicians use one's own mouthpiece and reed. Well, I'm still here to tell the tale.

I let Jimmy take my alto and I changed to baritone. As far as I'm concerned, it was a tremendous night and one I shall never forget. In recent years I have been told that Jimmy Dorsey did not extemporise and that he always wrote out his solos in advance. I can vouch for the fact that on that night at least he ad libbed like crazy![9]

Some time later, the club was raided one night. To get around the law, which prohibited the sale of alcohol after 2.00 a.m., the management served liquor after time in tea and

[8] Clarinettist Ted Lewis first brought his band from America to play at the Kit Kat restaurant in 1925 and made several return visits in the following years. He was well known for his catch-phrase question to the audience, 'Is everybody happy?'. Leading bands for some fifty years, he specialised in comedy, novelty and sentimental songs and show tunes but he employed jazz musicians such as Brunies and Spanier on a long term basis and included jazz in his shows (Ed.).

[9] Dorsey was in his mid-twenties when he sat in at the Melton Club. He would go on to lead one of the most successful American dance bands of the late 1930s and early 1940s (Ed.).

coffee pots, with cups and saucers on the tables. But the police had got to know about this, and had the place watched. Some officers in plain clothes were admitted and served with the evidence! Suddenly, by a pre-arranged plan, two lines of uniformed police marched in, going around the room to each table. All of the customers, together with the management and the waiters who had served the booze were taken away, and the club was closed. The band was allowed to go home.

We weren't long out of a job. Vic Filmer was a real go-getter and knew a lot of people in town. In two weeks we were playing at the Mitre Club in Mitre Court off Regent Street, an establishment that later became the Edmundo Ros Club. While we were working there, Vic negotiated a long contract for us with Murrays Club in Beak Street, also near Regent Street.

The job at Murrays, during 1930-31, gave me a lot of experience of a new kind. We had to play a nightly programme which included jazz and involved us in accompanying artistes such as Douglas Byng and Ben Blue. There were great dance routines choreographed by the famous Buddy Bradley. Some of the dancers at Murrays became film stars and two of these I remember were Googie Withers and Honor Blair.

A Vocal Trio

I was still studying orchestration at college during the day and, as my arranging experience developed, Vic introduced me to bandleaders such as Hal Swain who wanted arrangements for recording. I was also beginning to get known among musicians and soon I was getting offers to join other bands, but I stayed with Vic until the Murrays job folded.

Among the musicians in Vic Filmer's band was the drummer-vocalist-xylophonist Sid Plummer, and trumpeter Tommy Band, both of whom also played weekends at the Palace Hotel,

Southend-on-Sea. They introduced me to Tolchard Evans, a conductor-composer who had the band there. So I also began to work at weekends with his orchestra, which played a mix of musical styles. Tommy was a fine trumpet player but he could not play jazz and was only suitable for the overtures and classical pieces. After I started working with the orchestra I recommended Les Lambert for the jazz trumpet chair.[10]

I had met Les through Les Osborne, who at that time was managing the orchestral side of the music publishers Campbell and Connelly. Although the bulk of the repertoire consisted of popular songs of the day and light orchestral music with a little comedy on the side, Tolch badly needed someone to play jazz, so Les Lambert got the job. I knew that Les could sing, so we formed a vocal trio, bringing Sid Plummer into the team, which added to the entertainment. One number we did with tongue in cheek was called 'We're happy when we're hiking', in which we stood with trouser legs rolled up to the knee, back-packs on our shoulders and boy scout hats on our heads. We got an enormous audience reaction, from which I learned that you could get away with almost anything if you did it well and with sincerity.

At the same time, gigs were coming along via Ivor Mairants, who was working with a society bandleader and drummer named Marius B. Winter.[11] Ivor and I had been practising vocal duets and I suggested that Les Lambert should come in to make a trio. We listened to records by the Boswell Sisters and

---

[10] Les Lambert, who played piano as well as trumpet, was born in London in 1908 and had led his own band while still at school. He had worked with Alfredo and Marius Winter and with the house-band at Murray's Club. Later, like Harry Gold, he would become a key member of Roy Fox's orchestra (Ed.).

[11] Winter's main claim to fame seems to be that his dance band had been the first to broadcast on radio – on March 26th 1923 from the attic of Marconi House, London (Ed.).

the Rhythm Boys (Bing Crosby and Co.), from which our vocal group, the Cubs, developed its style when we joined Roy Fox's orchestra much later.

Ivor started to arrange the vocal trio parts and we rehearsed them in his parents' flat in Fieldgate Street in the East End of London. Some of the phrases were too difficult to sing at that early stage. By simplifying the most difficult ones at rehearsal we soon arrived at a system of mutual understanding. The more we rehearsed, the better we became, and we were able to sing some very complicated phrases.

At that time Annie and I occupied a two roomed flat in Commercial Road in the East End. To say it was 'crummy' (lousy) would be putting it mildly. I knew the drummer Maurice Burman[12] and learned that a flat was available in Maurice's parents' house in Amhurst Road, Stamford Hill. We moved there but my wife became pregnant and, as there was no room for a larger family at the Burmans' we found a flat in the same road, opposite their house.

Ivor, Les and I were doing a lot of gigs for Marius Winter, including regular performances on the roof garden at Selfridges store, in Oxford Street, playing for teas and dancing. Incredible as it may sound, we dressed up as minstrels, complete with wigs and with our faces blacked with burnt cork. It wasn't so bad putting on the black make-up but getting it off was another matter, particularly as we didn't have a dressing room.

Some months later, when I was dressed up in my dinner suit and ready to go to a gig with Marius, Annie started in labour. The landlady of the house called the doctor who ordered me away. Worrying about getting to the gig in time and about

---

[12] Maurice Burman had been working with Sam Costa in 1929 and led a band of his own the following year. Later he would work with Edgar Jackson's Band (led by Harry Gold) and then mainly with Roy Fox's orchestra (alongside Harry) during much of the 1930s (Ed.).

what was happening in the bedroom, I waited outside for what seemed an eternity until suddenly I heard a baby's cry. After waiting for a long time without getting any information, I knocked on the door. The landlady came out and declared, "You can't go in but I can tell you that you have a son." I had to leave then or be late for the gig, which was a little way out of London. Naturally, at the earliest opportunity I phoned, almost out of my mind with worry, only to discover that I had become the father of twin boys – Morton and Leslie. It seems that nobody knew there were two – not even the doctor! Needless to say, the band did Bacchus proud and Marius' usual wide smile got wider by the glass.

The Spider's Web

One day early in 1932 Maurice Burman phoned me to say that there was an opening for a band in a venue called the Spider's Web, which was a roadhouse situated on the Watford By-pass. Edgar Jackson was setting up a small band there. He had been at one time the Editor of the *Melody Maker* and had been its founder as a house magazine for Lawrence Wright, the music publisher. Edgar was a close friend of Maurice, who had told him about the vocal trio that Ivor, Les and I had put together. The four of us were engaged by Edgar to play at the Spider's Web, joined by a young pianist named Jack Nathan.[13]

Jack was a semi-pro who worked during the day at an accountant's office. Because of this, Les Lambert gave Jack the initials 'SPDW' (meaning 'Semi-pro Daily Worker') after his name. Les was what we called an 'arch-lumberer'. A

---

[13] London-born Jack Nathan was 21 at the time and had been playing piano from the age of five. The Spider's Web engagement was his breakthrough into work as a professional musician. Later he would work alongside Harry in Jack Padbury's and Roy Fox's bands (Ed.).

lumberer was someone who played practical jokes – 'lumbers', often with considerable embarrassment to the person lumbered, and Les was dedicated to lumbering. There were many instances of that kind of activity which I'll describe later. Les also had an eye for the main chance, which created a situation at the Spider's Web which resulted in our getting fired. He approached the management behind Edgar Jackson's back in an attempt to get the band engaged directly by the management and so avoid paying commission to Edgar. *C'est la vie!*

The five of us in Edgar Jackson's Band became great friends, always staying in the same digs whenever possible and becoming almost like the inseparable 'Famous Five' in the boys' stories about Greyfriars School. Maurice and I were particularly close, our friendship dating from the time when I lived in his parents' house in Stamford Hill. He had a sister, Alma, who started a variety and band agency with Lord Ulick Brown. He was a socialite who frequented the clubs and Alma eventually married him and became Lady Brown. I read with some amazement much later that, around that time, *The Times* newspaper had announced a forthcoming marriage between "Lord Ulick Brown and 'Elma' [sic] Warren, daughter of Colonel Burmanski of the Imperial Russian Army". I suppose it would have been considered *infra dig*, completely beneath his standing, for a Lord of the Realm to marry the daughter of a cobbler, which in fact Alma's father was. You certainly can't believe all you read in the newspapers, even in *The Times*. What is more surprising is that Lord Brown was a tall, handsome figure of a man, while Alma was not exactly a raving beauty. She must have had something other than looks that attracted him. For me, one important connection with that saga is that, later on, I got several gigs for my Pieces of Eight via Alma's agency.

The loss of the Spider's Web job caused a temporary parting of the ways, but soon, apart from Maurice, we were together again. We had created more than a little interest with the Spider's Web performances and we were offered a job to play in the Princes Restaurant in Piccadilly under the leadership of Jack Padbury. Jack played alto sax and clarinet so it became necessary for me to change to tenor sax. I still had the clarinet, soprano and baritone (as well as the stored bass saxophone, not required) which occasionally proved useful because I included their voices in the arrangements I scored for the band.

Jack Padbury was a very kind person and the band developed into a fine team, full of enthusiasm. Other members included Johnny Cantor on violin and Charlie Knapp on drums. Much of what we played was purely commercial music suitable for dancing but occasionally Jack would put on a short jazz set. Johnny Cantor would be included because he could play jazz, but not Jack, who recognised his shortcomings in that direction. The job was a good one and no doubt it could have lasted a long time, but fate decreed otherwise.

The band was popular with the clientele and many well-known visitors came to listen, including Louis Armstrong (who gave me a signed photo).[14] Among these visitors were Roy Fox, Edgar Jackson and Maurice Burman. Perhaps it would be more factual to say that Roy and Edgar had been brought in by Maurice, who had been informed that Roy was rebuilding his band, having lost the personnel at the Monseigneur Restaurant.

By that time Ivor, Les and I had developed the vocal trio to a highly polished state of proficiency and that interested Roy as much as our instrumental playing ability. It was obvious that Roy Fox was listening intently. Jack Padbury caught sight of

[14] This was during Armstrong's first playing visit to Britain, an event of immense significance for jazz in this country. He opened at the Palladium in London on July 18th 1932 and then toured with a group including saxophonists Harry Hayes and Buddy Featherstonhaugh and trumpeter Bruts Gonella. After working on the Continent he returned to London to play at the Holborn Empire in the summer and autumn of 1933 (Ed.).

Roy, Edgar and Maurice and said, "I hope he's not after you lads," which made us feel very uncomfortable because we knew that Roy was there for just that purpose.[15]

[15] Cornettist Roy Fox, born in Denver, Colorado in 1901 and raised in Hollywood, had been leading bands since 1920. He worked in New York, Miami and Hollywood during the 1920s and became musical director of Fox Film Studio in 1928. In 1930 he accepted an invitation to come to Britain to form a band at the Café de Paris in London and began broadcasting and recording for Decca the following year. When Fox became ill in October 1931 while working with his band at the Monseigneur Restaurant in Piccadilly, Lew Stone, his pianist and arranger, took over as leader. The following year, Stone was invited by the management to form his own band. The personnel he recruited was (but for the absence of trumpeter Sid Buckman) identical to Fox's (Ed.).

3.

THE ROY FOX ORCHESTRA AND HIGH SOCIETY

The popular dance bandleader Roy Fox had been recuperating in Switzerland after a long and serious illness in the autumn of 1931. While he was away, Lew Stone, who was Roy's pianist and arranger, held the fort with tremendous success, having changed the character of the band into a real swinging outfit. Under Lew's direction the band was getting film studio work and recording sessions and had become tremendously popular with the patrons. When Roy returned, the Monseigneur Restaurant management decided not to re-employ Fox as musical director. So it was necessary for him to rebuild his band, because most of the musicians wanted to stay with Stone, given the extra work they were getting. The exception was Sid Buckman, who played the 'whispering cornet' style previously created by Roy.[1]

A 'Big Time' Band

As I said earlier, Jack Padbury was a great guy to work for and the four of us (Ivor, Les, Jack Nathan and I) knew that if we left it would be the end of the road for the band at the Princes Restaurant, which incidentally has changed its name four times since then.

---

[1] Fox was known as 'the whispering cornettist' as much for his sweet-toned playing style as for his use of 'Whispering' as his signature tune (Ed.).

Regretfully for Jack, but pleasingly for us, we got the job and the five were reunited. We had now (it was towards the end of 1932) arrived at the 'big time' because Roy Fox already had a big reputation.[2] A rehearsal for the new orchestra was arranged in the Café Anglais in Leicester Square, where we would be performing for the following few months. There we met the rest of the band.

Rex Owen was lead alto sax and also featured clarinet, soprano sax, baritone sax and flute.[3] I had met Rex in 1929 when he was in the Fred Elizalde band at the Savoy, playing alongside Adrian Rollini. Hughie Tripp was the second alto and also played clarinet, baritone sax, ocarina and 'hot fountain pen' (an ebonite six-holed wind instrument which had been invented and played by Rollini). I had met Hughie when I worked with the Metronomes in Southampton, so I already had some friends in the saxophone section. The section was completed by Johnnie Walker on baritone sax and clarinet and myself on tenor and clarinet. From that time I became known as a tenor sax player.

The brass section comprised Les Lambert, lead trumpet and jazz soloist, Sid Buckman (sharing lead with Les) and Eric Tann, trombone. The rhythm section had Jack Nathan and Peggy Dell, pianos, Ivor Mairants, guitar, Maurice Burman on drums and George Gibbs playing double bass and sousaphone. Ivor also sometimes played the Hawaiian guitar, which we called the 'wanking iron'![4]

---

[2] Fox's first British major band, at the Monseigneur from the spring of 1931, had included stars such as trumpeter Nat Gonella and vocalist-guitarist Al Bowlly. Its regular weekly BBC radio broadcasts and Fox's Decca records, often featuring Bowlly's singing, were very popular. Fox's new band, including Harry Gold, opened at the Café Anglais on October 24th 1932 (Ed.).

[3] Owen remained with Roy Fox until August 1937. Later he worked with Bert Firman, Geraldo and Carroll Gibbons among many other bands (Ed.)

[4] Ivor Mairants worked with the Fox band until August 1937. Afterwards

George was the 'old man' of the band, being in his mid-forties. He was an ardent admirer of the mammary gland and always in search of highly developed ones. Whenever he spotted something truly gargantuan he would kick the back of his bass and the rest of us soon learned where to look by the direction of his head.

Apart from being a pianist, Peggy Dell, who hailed from Dublin, was also the band's singer, soon to be joined by Jack Plant. Jack had a vocal range similar to Morton Downey, the Irish tenor (after whom one of my sons is named). He could sing in quite a high register for a man. To hear him on radio, one could easily become convinced that the name was Jacqueline Plant. Peggy was a female baritone and, apart from the fact that Jack always appeared to be making love to the microphone, with his crooning style, I had to exercise utmost control to check an almost irresistible urge to laugh whenever they sang duets. Try to imagine it if you can. There was this slim, short, male soprano and this hefty female baritone singing love songs, male and female ranges coming out of the wrong mouths. On one occasion I failed to control the urge to laugh, which earned me a severe warning from Roy.

My seat in the placing of the band at the Café Anglais was close to the waiters' hot plate which was heated by methylated spirits. It had the effect of drawing oxygen from the immediate vicinity, and almost invariably around midnight my eyes would begin to close for a second or two. Subconsciously, I would

---

he had a long association with Geraldo's orchestra, freelanced, ran a dance music school and a jazz youth orchestra, taught music, and opened his own music shop in London. Nathan, Lambert and Burman were with Fox until the band broke up in August 1938. After the war Nathan worked with Harry Hayes and others and successfully led his own dance bands. After leaving Fox, Lambert worked regularly with various other bands until the early 1940s and afterwards successfully freelanced in studios and theatre orchestras. Burman worked with various bands in the 1940s, including Jack Nathan's and Geraldo's, ran a singing school and became a columnist for *Melody Maker* (Ed.).

continue playing and would suddenly become conscious of my surroundings again with a startled look in Roy's direction. To my knowledge, he never noticed.

We began broadcasting regularly from the Café on Wednesday nights, live for an hour and a half from 10.30 p.m. to midnight, and the band became known as one of the three top bands of the time. The others were Bert Ambrose and Lew Stone.

Apart from Peggy Dell and Jack Plant, Sid Buckman also sang songs with the band. He had a voice suitable for cowboy-type numbers like 'Home on the Range'. Les, Ivor and myself were now firmly established as a vocal trio. Roy chose to call the trio 'The Cubs', a connotative title suggested by the name Fox. We were paid £15 a week, plus extra for broadcasting and recording. Jack Nathan and I were also paid for orchestrations, though the money for these came from music publishers.

The Kit Kat

One night at the Café Anglais Roy told us that the band would be moving to the Kit Kat restaurant.[5] I immediately recalled the time when I was with Vic Filmer, and Jimmy Dorsey had played at the side of me when he was working at the Kit Kat with Ted Lewis. I fantasised a little, wondering if I would be sitting in his chair. Sounds silly, doesn't it? – but that's what it meant to me at the time.

A special rostrum had been built in three tiers at the Kit Kat, to accommodate the newly enlarged band, which now had four saxes and four brass, the rhythm section remaining the same as at the Café. In addition, another male singer, Denny Dennis,

[5] The Fox band opened at the Kit Kat on January 16th 1933 and remained in residence there for just over a year (Ed.).

was recruited. Denny was a fine singer who at times out-Crosbied Bing. He was a naive young fellow from Derby (his real name was Dennis Pountain) and he would fall, time and time again, for Les Lambert's lumbers. It was much like sending the apprentice to get 'striped paint' or a 'rubber centre punch' – the kind of thing that happened frequently in factory stores. It got so that most of us took part in the schoolboy-style practical jokes on Dennis. Looking back now I feel embarrassed about many of the tricks we played, but at the time we all thought it was great fun. More of that later.

While we were at the Kit Kat, Roy engaged a multi-instrumentalist named Art Christmas to play lead alto.[6] Rex Owen was relegated to the second chair. Art was a fine musician. He was also a bit of a comedian, which came in useful when, some time later, we went on tour in variety. However, we were to make another change before that.

In some ways, moving from the Café Anglais to the Kit Kat was a step down the social ladder in that the former was visited by an evening dress clientele while the latter, a much larger place, attracted a more general public. My preference was for the Kit Kat audiences, who were more down to earth and very enthusiastic. It was while we were at the Kit Kat that I renewed acquaintance with my old friend Joe Loss. His band was playing in the Capitol Cinema situated above the Kit Kat and it also played relief for our band in the Kit Kat.[7] So in the change over I was often able to have a quick chat with him.

[6] Canadian-born Art Christmas played brass and percussion instruments as well as reeds. He came to Britain in 1925 and worked extensively on the Continent in the late 1920s, leading his own band in Budapest and Berlin. After a year and a half with Percival Mackey's band, he was with Roy Fox from March 1933 until the breakup of the band in 1938. He worked mainly with Jack Payne in the 1940s, ran a pub in Hackney in the 1950s and later moved back to Canada (Ed.)

[7] After working at the Astoria with a seven-piece band, Loss had moved to the Kit Kat in 1931, and stayed there as resident bandleader for three years (Ed.).

My maternal grandparents, David and Rebecca Schulman. They were east London tobacco traders.

My parents, Sam and Hetty. Sam wasn't a trained musician but he loved music and used to sing operatic arias while working in his tailor's shop.

The Florentine Dance Band, c.1921. Left to right: HG, saxophone, clarinet; Ivor Mairants, banjo, guitar; Reg Smith, violin; Harry Atkins, saxophone; Harry Marco, drums; Bert Pearlstone, piano.

The real beginning of my professional career. Drayson Marsh's London Dance Band, Lewisham Dance Lounge, 1924. Left to right: Harold Watson, piano; Dennis Powell, banjo, guitar; Phil Cork, drums, violin; Francis Watson, trumpet; HG, reeds. We were a co-operative with Phil as leader.

Shanklin Pier, Isle of Wight, Summer 1926. Left to right: Phil Cork, Harold Watson, Dennis Powell, HG, Francis Watson. Still the Drayson Marsh personnel but by now we had won prizes and some acclaim, and Phil had changed our name to 'The Metronomes'.

Marius Winter's band, Selfridges Roof Garden, London, c.1931. Marius is on the left. Ivor Mairants is holding the guitar. I'm on his left, with the alto saxophone. How we could play, dressed up like that, I don't know.

'Big time' at last! The Roy Fox Orchestra, one of the two or three top British dance orchestras of its day, in the early 1930s. Left to right: Johnnie Walker, George Gibbs, Les Lambert, Eric Tann, Maurice Burman, Jack Nathan, Rex Owen, Sid Buckman, Jack Plant, Hughie Tripp, Ivor Mairants, HG, Roy Fox.

Roy Fox's 'Cubs', c.1934. Ivor Mairants, Les Lambert and me.

Roy Fox Orchestra at Croydon Airport, early 1933, en route for the Continent to give a command performance for the King of the Belgians. Left to right: Maurice Burman, Eric Tann, Jack Nathan, HG, Sid Buckman, Dorothy Fox, Roy Fox, pilot, Jack Plant, Johnnie Walker, Ivor Mairants, Rex Owen, Hughie Tripp, George Gibbs.

The Fox Orchestra on a stage set, mid-1930s. I am nearest to the camera. Next to me are Hughie Tripp and Art Christmas. The singer is Mary Lee.

Roy Fox and his orchestra, mid-1930s. Left to right: Eric Tann (tbn), Jack Nathan (p), Miff Ferrie (tbn), Sid Buckman (tpt), Les Lambert (tpt), Ivor Mairants (g), Ronnie Genarder (g, vcl), Andy Hodgkiss (tpt), Maurice Burman (dms), Roy Fox, Jack Plant (vcl), Rex Owen (saxes), George Gibbs (b), Art Christmas (reeds), HG (reeds), Peggy Dell (p, vcl), Hughie Tripp (reeds).

Oscar Rabin (inset) and The Oscar Rabin Band, early 1940s. Oscar and Harry Davis are at the microphone. The sax section is (left to right) Harry Conn, Johnny Swinfen, HG and Benny Keen. Trumpeter Bix Benstead is behind Harry Conn. Cecil Laley-Walden is on drums and Bill Whinnie on bass. Pianist Eddie Palmer sits next to the massive novachord. It sounded beautiful but it nearly broke our backs when we had to lift it

West Indian Christmas
Party broadcast, December
15th, 1944. Left to right:
singers Neville Taylor, Ida
Shepley, Edric Connor and
Rita Williams, and HG. I
was leading the regular
band on the BBC's West
Indian Party broadcasts at
the time (photo courtesy of
BBC Picture Archive).

With Belgian bandleader
Peter Packay in Brussels,
spring 1945. After the
Normandy landings I went
with Eric Winstone's band
to the Continent, helping to
entertain the troops.

Liberation! VE (Victory in
Europe) Day, Paris, May
1945. With John Arslanian
on the Champs Élysées.
Later that day our band
broadcast for the BBC
from the grounds of the
British Embassy.

American friends: (top left) Adrian Rollini, my mentor on bass sax, in the 1920s (photo courtesy of Tom Faber); (top right) Louis Armstrong at the time of his 1932-3 visits to Britain; (bottom left) Hoagy Carmichael - a memento of the great 1948 concert (E. A. Bachrach photo); (bottom right) Spencer Williams, my song-writing partner for a time and the composer of 'Basin Street Blues'.

On New Year's Eve I fell into Roy Fox's bad books as a result of a suggestion by Miff Ferrie, the trombone player who had been added to the brass section. Being a Scot he thought it was a great idea for us to drink each other's health at midnight. Unfortunately, however, this would be while we were still on the stand. We agreed to have a miniature bottle of whisky handy and at a suitable moment close to midnight we would take a quick sip. Roy was generally pleasant and always acted the gentleman but, unluckily for me, he turned from facing the audience in time to catch me taking a swig. Apart from the fact that he was a non-drinker himself, he had laid down a rule that we should not drink on the stand. At that moment, as I was gripping the little whisky bottle, I saw a different side to Roy's character. He didn't raise his voice but the look I got from him registered sheer hatred. Of course, in the interval I went over and apologised. He accepted the apology with the warning that next time it would be instant dismissal.

The Kit Kat management put on a cabaret show every week. Among the performers in one of the cabarets was a instrumental comedy double act. At rehearsal they asked if anyone would like a car. They wanted to dispose of it. It was unreliable and used too much petrol, but, of course, they didn't tell us that. Apart from Denny Dennis and myself everyone in the band already had a car. One of the partners in the cabaret act said, "We'll take a saxophone in exchange for it." They wanted to include the saxophone in their act. I decided I would have the car so I went along to Lewin Brothers where I bought a brass alto sax for twenty five pounds. On Saturday night, the night of the last performance of their show, I was asked to go with them to their home in Acton. They would leave their stage props there and I would leave the alto for them and bring away the car. The only problem was that I couldn't drive, so Eric Tann offered to travel with us and show me how to drive. Denny Dennis was staying in our house in Stamford Hill at the time, so he came too.

Once we had taken possession of the car Eric got into the driver's seat, I sat beside him to watch and Denny sat in the back. Off we went from Acton all the way to the Embankment that runs alongside the River Thames. Eric brought the car to a halt. He got out and moved to the front passenger seat while I got into the driver's seat. Then came information on the use of the clutch, gears, accelerator and brake pedal. The car was a Hillman 16-horsepower saloon and rather large for someone only 5'2" tall. Also, it had a gate change gearbox with the gear lever on the right of the driver. It was necessary to learn the technique of double de-clutching because this was before synchromesh gearboxes had been invented.

I managed to use the gears without crashing them and drove along the Embankment at twenty miles an hour until Eric told me to stop, which was exactly opposite a garage where he had parked his own car. He got out, telling me "You can drive it home from here, you're OK." There was nothing else to do but get Denny to guide me – a case of the blind leading the blind! Off we went and miraculously I managed to change gears, stop at police controlled junctions while keeping the engine running, and move on when motioned to do so by the officer on duty. I had no driving licence or insurance, which would have got me into trouble if I had been unable to keep going.

When we reached the turn off to the road where we lived, Denny suggested I should drive around for a while for practice. After an hour of this he suggested I should turn the car around using my reverse gear. "What's that?" I said. Eric hadn't said anything about a reverse gear. The upshot was that I couldn't find out how to reverse. Denny and I both had to get out to turn the car around by hand, pushing backwards and forwards until we got it in the right position and could set off for home.

The following morning, which was a Sunday so there was little traffic, I managed to find the reverse gear and celebrated by going for a drive. I gained more confidence and on Monday morning decided to drive to the West End. "Where ignorance is bliss, 'tis folly to be wise!" I must have been born under a lucky star. There was no mishap and as far as I know I didn't do anything wrong. I called at the Astoria in Charing Cross Road, where the Metronomes started. I thought I would call on Phil Cork who had been leader of the Metronomes and was now leading his own band there. He asked me to give him a lift in the car to Oxford Circus and when he got out he asked how long I had been driving. When I told him he said with feeling, "Fuckin' 'ell, if I'd known that I'd never 'ave got into the bleedin' thing."

Café de Paris

Following a successful season at the Kit Kat, we left to go to the Café de Paris in Leicester Square, a prestigious venue frequented by the highest of high society.[8] It was a real top hat, white tie and tails place. In a way we felt it was a bit of a 'leg-up' because it had been a famous West End spot since time immemorial. The dance floor was tiny and very few dancers could be accommodated. Nevertheless, it would be full of couples moving cheek to cheek, one foot chasing the other in a meaningless slouch, not always in tempo but, certainly to those on the dance floor, enjoyable. The Café de Paris was not as large as the Kit Kat, but it was larger than the Café Anglais and included a balcony on three sides of the room.

Among the regular customers were the Duke and Duchess of Kent and, even more frequently, Edward, Prince of Wales, complete with entourage and lady friends. They had their regular table in a corner to the right of the band. It was there

---

[8] The Fox band's residency at the Café de Paris lasted from March 5th to May 19th 1934 (Ed.)

that I saw for the first time something new in men's evening wear – a dinner jacket with a white waistcoat and a shirt with a soft collar, introduced by the Prince and starting a new fashion.

The cabaret was the main attraction, being assembled from the best artistes in the world, recruited from the Continent and America. The band took second place. We were only needed to accompany the acts or play for dancing after the show had ended. It was interesting to watch tables being brought from their hidden store to be placed on the dance floor as more and more customers came to be seated in time for the start of the cabaret. Panic-stricken waiters, under the eagle eye of the restaurant manager, rushed back and forth with chairs, tablecloths, glasses and cutlery until there was no space left for dancing. All the activity became even more noticeable when, at the end of the cabaret performance, people began leaving in droves, and once again the waiters rushed around removing tables and chairs to make way for dancing to resume.

It was a glamorous life-style for the people who went to the Café de Paris to enjoy themselves. I loved being inside that glittering world. Who wouldn't? We musicians came from ordinary backgrounds but our music gave us a way in to that society environment. But, at the same time, I was very conscious of the injustice of it all. There were many people at that time who had nothing. The divide between the haves and have-nots was very obvious. There was unemployment everywhere. I watched the rich patrons at the Café de Paris and thought about it all politically. It reinforced my socialist convictions.

Roy never came in for the first band set. We were left in the charge of Sid Buckman, who was accepted as the deputy leader. We had music pads containing printed commercial arrangements from which we played chorus after chorus with complete boredom. This was a system used by 'name' bandleaders in most of the restaurants and clubs. It was designed to show how good they were. As soon as Roy took the stand the printed commercial arrangements would be put aside and out would come the books with the specially orchestrated manuscript parts. The band would suddenly come alive. The music sounded much better and it proved to the management and to the customers how important the bandleader was. An excellent psychological ploy.

We musicians were treated very well by the management and staff, receiving good meals and being allowed to go to the dispense bar and buy any drink for six pence (2½p). I was delighted to have the chance to see some of the cabaret acts because of my interest in the theatre engendered by frequent visits to shows in my young days. There was Sophie Tucker and Leslie Hutchinson (the singer at the piano, not the trumpeter Leslie 'Jiver' Hutchinson). And I loved Ben Blue's new act, having seen him some years previously in Murray's Club. At the Café de Paris, part of his act involved a stooge who stood well to the side holding a large block of ice while Ben, ignoring him, would be doing something else. The stooge kept coming forward asking "Now?" and Ben would say "Not yet", with the ice block steadily getting smaller. Eventually with the ice block almost gone Ben would say, "I don't need it now." I saw the same act performed later by Jimmy James when we went on tour.

What has all this to do with the Pieces of Eight? Let me explain before I carry on with this history. I was learning how to do it in the school of experience; working out how to put my own music together and present it.

When I was with the Metronomes I was beginning to get a feeling about the direction I wanted to go musically. I found myself being misdirected by circumstances in the conditions of the various professional engagements. But it was precisely that which gave me some insight into what I was aiming at, even if only in small doses.

Working in the Fox band gave a great deal of relevant experience. At the same time, it gave me the money I needed to further my musical education and keep the family. And it planted in me subconsciously the idea of setting up a small jazz band. Most of the arrangements I was writing for Roy's band – although they were arrangements for a big band – were in the jazz idiom.

On October 13th 1934, the *Melody Maker* printed a piece under the headline 'Hunters of the Fox' which discussed Jack Nathan's work and mine as arrangers for the Fox band. After suggesting that 'Nathan and Gold' sounded a bit like the name of a comedy act it went on to praise Jack's arranging ability. Justifiably so. He did all the ballad arrangements and the special concert style scores, including a development of Roy's signature tune 'Whispering' as a symphonic kind of piece. And Jack's vocal accompaniments were superb. In fact, after leaving Fox, he became a well-known bandleader in his own right in hotels and clubs in London's West End. The *Melody Maker* article also made clear that "Gold is responsible for most of Roy Fox's swing arrangements." For example, I arranged the jazz piece 'Hunting the Fox' which Maurice Burman had written for the band. It was obvious where my heart lay – with jazz – albeit that the music I was involved with then with Roy was a far cry from the Original Dixieland Jazz Band, which I had first heard, or from Bix, Trumbauer, Nichols, Venuti, Lang, Rollini and the others that had come later.

While we were at the Café de Paris, Roy called a meeting during an interval one evening and made the following announcement: "Boys, we're going on tour. Think about it and let me know who doesn't want to go." With that, he left the bandroom to give us the opportunity to discuss it. Les Lambert, in his most exuberant, high spirited manner, shouted out one word – 'Kife', which was understood to mean 'women and sex'. We took him to task, pointing out that it was important to discuss how much pay we should need, bearing in mind that we would spend a lot of time travelling and there would be the costs of living in hotels and other economic needs, apart from expenses at home. We finally agreed that we would need at least an extra £3 a week. We put that to Roy and he agreed without objection. In retrospect Ivor Mairants and I thought we should have asked for more – we would have got it, to be sure.

A Touring Band

However, touring with the Fox band[9] proved to be a cornerstone in developing my musical experience and in my discovery of an outlet for combining music with entertainment. At first, we travelled in a coach hired by Roy, but he almost always travelled in his Rolls Royce, accompanied by his wife Dorothy and his wife's maid, and driven by a chauffeur. We, of course, looked for the best digs we could find, which were usually recommended by the stage manager or stage-door keeper in the various theatres at which we played. They were cheap and the food was mostly good. The landladies would either shop for food and cook our meals, or they would cook whatever we brought in. There would be a bedroom and the communal use of a sitting room. Including cleaning services and cooking the cost was usually around three pounds. Laundry was done by arrangement at the theatres with a service that collected early in the week and returned in time for our departure to the next town.

Over the years, while I was working in touring bands, living in digs became something of a way of life for me. Some time

---

[9] Roy Fox's band undertook its first nationwide theatre tour in May 1934 and continued the pattern of touring until the final break-up of the band in August 1938 (Ed.).

after my period with Roy Fox, the Musicians Social and Benevolent Council, at my instigation, began to collect the addresses of the best digs in various towns, as recommended by musicians who had stayed in them. Sometimes people refused to share the information, but in general the scheme worked well. So I often found myself staying in the same digs with musicians from other bands who were working in the same town. That gave us a good chance to exchange stories over a drink or three.

Of course, there are lots of stories musicians like to tell about landladies. I heard one from Tommy McQuater, the trumpeter, while I was in digs with some of the Scottish personnel of the famous Squadronaires band. They had been staying at a boarding house where the landlady had a 'touch of the thirst'. They had bought a bottle of sherry to be sipped before their meals and had left it on display. After a day or so the level in the bottle seemed to be getting lower and they realised that their hostess was also taking a drop or two of the amber liquid. Drastic retaliatory action was decided on and a small amount of urine was introduced into the bottle. The level on Saturday, the day of departure, just before their final meal, was lower still. At the meal, the landlady, beaming, brought in her culinary triumph. "Well gentlemen," she said, "As it's your last meal this week, I've made you a nice trifle for your dessert. I've used some of your sherry. I hope you don't mind." Tommy didn't say what happened then.

Touring with Roy Fox I often found myself in the same digs as a well-known comic or a performer from one of the other acts on the bill. It was tremendous fun after the show to be drinking with people like that and hearing gags and getting information about show business, which became stored in my mind. Our performances were geared to audiences used to variety, which meant that ideas had to be forthcoming for comedy and stage presentation. All the music had to be memorised which meant long rehearsals at first. But gradually we became adept at memorising the arrangements, to the extent that a new arrangement could be introduced into the show the same day it had been rehearsed. The trick was to try to see a picture of the music, as written out on the manuscript, in the mind's eye. It worked.

The experience in variety with the Fox band, and some years later with Oscar Rabin, stood me in good stead when I eventually formed my own band, the Pieces of Eight. My normal timorous attitude was transformed to create a stage personality. I even learned some simple 'tap' routines. Watching the wonderful comic acts from the wings on stage must have played its part in that development.

The acts included people like Max Wall, the Irish comedians Arthur Lucan and Kitty McShane, Dickie Henderson Sr., and Richard Hearne. There was the trio (two men and a woman) of Wilson, Keppel and Betty, who dressed (or undressed) like ancient Egyptians for their routine and were excellent tap dancers. Murray and Mooney (later Mooney and King) were famous for their catch-phrase "I don't wish to know that; kindly leave the stage." And there was the hilarious Jimmy James and his singing lighthouse keeper (later joined by Roy Castle). I used to watch these performers' acts twice nightly, taking it all in to the point where I knew every move, and particularly their timing. Timing! How important that is! These entertainers knew to a split second the time from the opening bars of their play-on music to the point when they should be centre stage.

Mind you, although on stage the performers in the double acts would appear to be great friends, in some cases the opposite would be true off stage. Murray and Mooney would row constantly. I stayed in the same digs with them on more than one occasion when the language was 'flowery' and the shouting could be heard three streets away. Lucan and McShane were similarly inclined and, as for the Irish boxer-singer Jack Doyle, he would introduce his 'dear lovely lady wife Movita' with such loving charm. But after leaving the stage at the end of the act he would sometimes have a fight with her that looked like one of his bouts in the ring, except that he stayed on his feet. I should explain that he was a handsome heavyweight who always seemed to end his fights – other than with his wife – on the floor.

Generally, the Fox band was a friendly and happy environment. We worked hard because we enjoyed what we were doing, in spite of the odd niggle – inevitable in a group of people always together. The situation changed slightly when we decided to ask Roy to let us travel in our own cars. He agreed with the proposal and, because he could now dispense with the coach, gave us a petrol allowance.

We made a bit on the side by teaming up, so two band members might share some expenses. We also took turns in using each other's cars, thus saving wear and tear. That didn't always work out if someone else's wife or girlfriend came along. We also had a football team and would try to get a game in the various towns where we performed. I, being fleet of foot, played outside right, while George Gibbs and Les Lambert (both heavies) were backs. I don't remember the rest of the team apart from Denny Dennis who was a good forward. I remember a time when we played against the Nottingham police and a second eleven in Edinburgh with a measure of success.

The musicians began to get disgruntled when Leslie MacDonnell, who later became one of the heads of the London Palladium, was engaged by Roy as manager. Leslie was a shrewd business man who was there to advise Roy on how to make more money and, at the same time, keep the members of the band sweet. He was always telling us how bad business was and made it clear that we couldn't get any increase in pay. It was difficult for me to connect the statement that business was bad with the fact that Roy would frequently show us diamond bracelets, rings and other valuable goodies that he had bought as gifts for his wife. Also he was an inveterate gambler, betting large sums on horse and dog races, and losing more often than winning.

Before we started touring in Britain we had gone abroad on three occasions. The first trip was a flight to Brussels to play at a command performance for the Belgian King Albert.[10] It was the first time most of us had flown and was quite a thrill. The plane was chartered from Imperial Airways and took off from Croydon Airport. It was a square-fuselaged crock of a biplane (which I always think of as being tied together with string) powered by twin-engines.

The second flight was to Paris for a broadcast in a special programme in the afternoon. That left us free for the night before flying back. The band split up into small groups looking for their own brand of entertainment. Ivor Mairants and I acted as guardians for Peggy Dell as we felt we couldn't leave her to fend for herself. We went to look for a restaurant and came across a cafe full of what we thought were beautiful women dressed in gorgeous evening gowns, drinking and dancing. But we soon realised they were males. In our innocence we were more than surprised. Neither Ivor nor I had known of gay people or transvestites. They were really something and in some cases more attractive than females I have known.

After a meal we tried to get back to the hotel, but were completely lost. Neither of us knew enough French to ask the way. Suddenly we heard an elderly couple speaking Yiddish, which I think of as basically German. Ivor, being very fluent in the language, stopped them to ask the way and we got back home safe and dry.

---

[10] According to Ivor Mairants (in *My Fifty Fretting Years*), "One night at the Café Anglais, a guest waltzing round the postage stamp dance floor asked Roy if he would like to take the band to Brussels to play for the King of the Belgians, and Roy thought it was a 'leg-pull'. But it turned out to be genuine..." (Ed.)

The return flight was a bit of a nightmare, however. While crossing the Channel we entered a very turbulent area during which the plane was subject to sudden hair-raising fast descents of a couple of hundred feet or more, leaving our stomachs up above. Andy Hodgkiss, one of the trumpet players, suggested a drop of whisky would be a good idea. He signalled to the stewardess, who brought large scotches. They seemed to settle us and after a while I got out of my seat with the intention of ordering another couple. But the stewardess, almost panic-stricken, urged me to go straight back to my seat. It was then I realised that we were in a snowstorm and losing height so much that I could see boats, much larger than they ought to be. We were almost on the surface of the sea, or so it seemed.

Deauville

The third voyage abroad (during a month's break from the Kit Kat in the summer of 1933) began with a tour of Belgium and Holland. That was immediately followed by two weeks in Deauville on the Normandy coast to play at the Casino where the wealthy summered and gambled. There was also a room in the Casino for poorer people, who could gamble the odd franc, and where I occasionally spent precisely that amount.

We travelled to Deauville by coach from Holland, arriving in the early hours of the morning with nowhere to stay. Roy, of course, had gone to his hotel which had been booked in advance. Les Lambert said he would investigate the situation and left the rest of us sitting in the coach, tired, hungry, cold and feeling like refugees. But after a while the coach door burst open violently and there was Les saying excitedly, "There's beer, food and JAZZ!" Although it was four in the morning, we moved like lightning to the café Les had found. While we were feeding our faces, we asked about the possibility of a place to stay, and were recommended to a pension which was walking distance from the Casino. It was more expensive than we had anticipated paying, but any port has to serve in a storm. And we were going to be provided with evening meals by the Casino management, so we looked for and found a very good restaurant – also expensive – nearby for lunches. What the hell, we thought; let's make it a holiday!

At night we played fifteen minute sets alternating with a fabulous Latin-American group led by a Cuban named Don Barreto. We were able to get drinks behind the bandstand and Maurice Burman, Ivor Mairants and I stayed to listen to Barreto's band. Maurice was inspired to write a piece for the Fox band in the Latin idiom which he called 'La Majestica'. In it Rex Owen played flute and soprano sax in emulation of one of the players in Barreto's group. Listening to them also helped me to arrange Latin-American music when later I went into music publishing. I wrote many arrangements in that style for Edmundo Ros while I was working for David Toff's organisation, because I had been able to hear at first hand how it should be done.[11]

There was also a cabaret with English dancing girls and naturally some of us, including me, got very friendly with them. As we came to the conclusion that they would not be highly paid, we wondered how they managed to survive with the high cost of living in the resort of Deauville. They told us they were staying in a bistro with full board for about a quarter of what we were paying. However 'there was no room at the

---

[11] Edmundo Ros, who spent his early life in Venezuela, came to Britain in 1937 and worked as a singer and percussionist with various Latin-styled bands including Don Barreto's. He led a very popular Latin-American dance band in Britain through the 1940s and 1950s, remaining active until the mid-1970s, made numerous records and broadcasts and opened his own club in London in 1949. Ivor Mairants (in *My Fifty Fretting Years*) remembers Barreto's group, comprising guitar, flute, piano, bass and percussion, as "without doubt years ahead of their time.... Had they existed today, they would have acquired an international reputation." (Ed.).

inn' so we had to make do with our accommodation in the pension. Les, Maurice, Jack Nathan and I did go to the bistro for lunches which by comparison with what we had been paying were ridiculously cheap and of excellent quality. One night after the show the four of us invited the ladies to stay in our digs, and they accepted. When I think of it now it seems a stupid situation. All four of us musicians were sharing a room. Obviously nothing could have happened other than sleep.

The following morning we had to organise breakfast for the girls as well as for us. We tossed a coin to decide who should tell the proprietress. I lost! Her English was as limited as my French. Full of embarrassment I asked her "Kannen sie Deutsch sprechen?" to which she replied "Ja". Then with much hesitation I explained the situation as delicately as possible. Much to my relief she didn't bat an eyelid. That's the French for you – very understanding.

Another incident, which to a self-conscious Briton like me was embarrassing at the time, occurred when Les, Maurice and I visited the toilet in the Casino, a luxurious place to be sure. A woman was in there cleaning with a cloth and brush. She just said "Bonjour" and went on with her work. What else could one do but ignore her. Not 'lumberer' Les Lambert. He opened up a conversation with her from his place at the urinal, so she promptly went over to where he was pissing, leaned over the partition and continued the conversation. It meant nothing to her. I suppose it was a case of 'when you've seen one you've seen them all.'

For the return to England Roy organised a coach to take us to Le Havre where we were to embark on a boat to Southampton. Walking to the harbour we passed some middle-aged women looking out of an open window and one of them shouted "Allo, Tommy!" Use your imagination!

That journey on the water was one of the worst any of us had experienced. The sea was very rough, and we were booked into a kind of dormitory for the night, with hard bunks and no linen. There must have been two hundred people trying to sleep there. It was stifling and some were being seasick all the time. Les and I decided it would be better to leave and find somewhere else to sit out the journey. Les found the telegraph operating room, where an obliging operator waving a bottle of whisky invited us to, "Come in and make yourselves comfortable." We didn't need a second invitation. We generously helped him out in downing frequently poured tots of whisky until the ship was approaching the mainland. With an agreeable feeling produced by the alcohol we bade a fond farewell and disembarked tired but happy.

Les's Lumbers

Touring with Roy meant, first of all, new band uniforms. He always insisted that we should wear uniforms rather than evening dress. They had to be provided at our own expense and were always required whenever we returned from our month's annual unpaid holiday in August. At a meeting, Roy would indicate the style and we all had to agree on the colour and kind of cloth. For example, one year we had dark blue uniforms in a kind of naval style, with brass buttons to look like gold, and epaulettes; another year the uniforms were white. Luckily, my father made my uniform at cost.

The first rehearsal before setting off on the road for the new season was a tedious operation. While we had been away new tunes had become popular, which meant memorising arrangements for the new show. Our rehearsals were usually called for eleven o'clock in the morning, but Ivor, Les and I started an hour earlier to rehearse our vocal parts. After rehearsal, the musicians would repair to the nearest hostelry for ale, bread, cheese and pickles.

Somehow, Sid Buckman always managed to arrive just as the last round of beer was being ordered. With unfailing regularity it was: "Hullo Sid, just in time. What'll it be?" We came to the conclusion that he hid himself behind a door to time his entrance precisely. Anyway we cooked his goose on that score. We planned that the next time he appeared in the pub after everyone else we would make way for him to get to the bar. As usual, he came in for the last shout and, like Moses parting the waters of the Nile, we made two lines and shouted in unison "It's your turn, Sid!" He bought a drink for the whole assembly and never came in again.

I've mentioned earlier some of Les Lambert's notorious lumbers. But perhaps it is worth mentioning a few more, mostly directed at Denny Dennis, but also one aimed at me and one at Maurice Burman.

Denny always seemed to be fair game and every word said in his hearing he would take with utmost seriousness. He was a fine singer with perfect phrasing and excellent intonation and was very popular with radio listeners. Consequently, whenever Denny was introduced on stage a roar of delight would erupt, with extended applause. But when he had finished his song the reaction was usually less enthusiastic because he couldn't sell himself on stage properly. The rest of us tried to develop Denny's personality in a genuinely friendly way. But not Les Lambert. He couldn't resist the temptation to lumber.

During that period a well-known cigarette manufacturing firm included, in its packets of cigarettes, picture cards of famous footballers demonstrating football action positions. One day, Les said to Denny, "It would be a really good idea if you collected those cards. Then you could practise the positions. It would help you to relax and develop your personality." Denny swallowed the suggestion, hook, line and sinker. From then on, to the great amusement of the rest of the band, he could be seen daily, practising shots at imaginary goals, or with arms outstretched saving them.

While Denny, Les and I and some of the others were staying together in the same digs during a week's engagement at the

Leeds Empire, the now famous 'Chestbrush Incident' occurred. The stories have been told over and over again by various people who were not present when it happened but pretended they were. Of course, they added the usual embellishments. I've heard those stories told by people who didn't know that I had actually been there when the celebrated 'incident' occurred, and I have had to correct the exaggerations.

Here is what really happened. Les Lambert, Jack Nathan, Denny, the trombonist George Rowe and I were sharing a large dormitory-type bedroom. Les made a bet with George that he could sell Denny a hairbrush which Les used for cleaning hair and dandruff from his comb. The brush had been bought from Woolworths for three shillings and sixpence and the selling price to Denny was to be five shillings (25p). Les and George bet a pound on it and agreed with a handshake.

Les prided himself on being an athlete and a fresh air fiend. One morning, he opened the bedroom window and stood by it taking deep breaths while beating his chest with the brush. After a few minutes, unable to contain himself, Denny said, "What's that for, Les?" Les replied, "I'm opening the pores of my skin. That allows the air to get through to my skin, which in turn gets to my lungs. It'll help my breathing for blowing the trumpet." After a few seconds he added, "It's also good for my singing with the Cubs."

Denny asked, "How much are those brushes?" "Five bob," said Les. More silence. Then from Denny, "Look Les, it's more important for me. Could you sell me that one and get another for yourself?" "Yes, of course," said Les, handing over the brush and pocketing the five shillings (and a pound from George). It was magnificently done.

The lumber aimed at me was in an entirely different category and executed in the very same digs the same week. Morning tea and the mail were usually brought into our room by the landlady. One morning she handed me a letter bearing a Leeds postmark. On opening it I found a letter addressed from 'St. Asaph's Home for Destitute Ladies, 215b Harrogate Road, Leeds'. It read:

> Dear Mr. Gold,
>   We have in our care a young lady with a baby which she claims you are the father. While I have no right to take sides in the matter, it would serve a useful purpose if you will kindly come here any morning to discuss with me what is your view and meet with the lady in person.
>   Yours faithfully, E. Hardcastle (Mrs.), Matron.

To say that I was flabbergasted would be the understatement of the century. I was struck dumb with fear. I had heard of lawsuits about paternity where, in most cases, the defendant lost.

In a panic I went to Les and showed him the letter. He said, "Harry, I think you're in trouble." "It's not possible," I said. "What do you think I should do?" "Go along and face the music," he replied. "Whatever you do, don't ignore it." I asked him to come with me but he refused, so off I went and walked up and down Harrogate Road, looking for number 215b. Eventually I realised that the address didn't exist and concluded that it was one of Lambert's famous lumbers. Well done, Les!

Then there was the lumber on Maurice Burman. We had been finishing an engagement at Yarmouth one Saturday night. We had our cars ready to drive on to Bournemouth next day for the Sunday concert there. After we had all set off, Maurice couldn't understand why there was a persistent smell of kippers cooking while he was driving. His car seemed full of the smell. Arriving in Bournemouth, the truth was revealed. It turned out that Les had bought a kipper in Yarmouth and carefully tied it to the exhaust pipe of Maurice's car. It had been cooking steadily throughout the journey.

There was another occasion I remember – I suppose you could say it was a lumber to get us out of trouble – when we had arrived to play an engagement at a theatre in Belfast. As usual, the 'Famous Five' (Ivor, Jack, Les, Maurice and I) turned up for the Monday morning rehearsal. There were crowds of people walking about and we stood outside the stage door idly watching the world go by, waiting for the door to be opened. Eventually someone came over to say that the stage door would not be opened until the evening as it was a bank holiday. We decided to find a pub en route to our digs which necessitated crossing Donegall Square. When we reached the other side of the square we were accosted by a group of local lads one of whom squared up to Ivor Mairants. "Protestant or Catholic?" he challenged. Ivor said, "I'm a Jew."

The lad hesitated and, looking nonplussed, repeated the question to each one us in turn. We each gave the same answer. We thought that discretion was the better part of valour in this situation. We left the scene without any trouble. No doubt the incident has given rise to the well worn joke, "Yes, but are you a Protestant Jew or a Catholic Jew?"

One final lumber on Denny Dennis that I'll mention took place during that same engagement in Belfast in our hotel one night after the show. Denny had become interested in spiritual phenomena and while we were sitting together in the lounge, he suggested that we should hold a seance. The rest of us told him that we weren't interested but his fanatical insistence finally persuaded us to agree. He arranged us in a circle around a table on which we were to lay our hands. Having seated us to his satisfaction, he started to ask the spirits repeatedly, "Is anyone there?" and finally, "If anyone is there, please knock twice."

After a long, boring silence which produced a few yawns and sniggers, I decided we should get some action. I whispered to Ivor, who was sitting next to me, that I was going to fake a trance. I laid back in my chair with my eyes closed. A few groans from me brought the desired reaction. Denny said, expectantly, "What was that?" Quick as a flash, Ivor

responded, "It's Harry. Either he's fainted or he's in a trance."
The others immediately realised what was going on and
displayed some interest. There was heavy breathing and some
unintelligible sounds from me. Denny was snared. He shouted
excitedly, "Quiet! This is marvellous. Let's listen." Then the
germ of an idea came to me. In a loud, guttural accent, I
rasped in German, "Ich bin Wagner." "What's he saying?"
Denny asked. "He's speaking German. He said he's Wagner,"
said Ivor. The rest of the group started to play along with
excited noises. Then with a strong foreign accent I said, "Jass,
she iss no moosick. Iss mutch noisse." At that, Denny came
forward, putting his face into mine, and said angrily, "Ain't
you never heard of Duke Ellington?"

That was too much. I was already in a state of subdued
merriment and ready to burst into unrestrained laughter. Out of
the corner of my mouth I told Ivor I was going to return to
normal. Les heard what I said and, with inspired presence of
mind, dipped his fingers into a nearby flower vase that was
almost full of water and put a few drops on my head to
simulate perspiration. My pretended recovery achieved, I
clearly heard Denny say, "You fucking bastard." It was then
that I discovered that, reposing in the centre of my forehead
and mixed with the water droplets, was a large green leaf.

Peggy

Soon after we started our long tour of Britain's variety theatres
an incident occurred that was to completely change my life.

Ivor Mairants, Les Lambert, Jack Nathan, Hughie Tripp and
I arrived in our cars outside the stage door of the Alhambra
Theatre in Bradford. We were to play there on a week's
engagement and were hoping to ask the stage manager for a
list of available theatrical digs. But we had arrived too late.

Rehearsals had ended and the door was closed until the evening performance.

We sat wondering disconsolately what our next move should be, when a lovely young blonde lady came up and asked, "Are you Roy Fox's band?" We said we were and asked her if she knew of any place where we could stay for the week. She said, "My friend Rita's mother has a commercial hotel but I don't know if there are any vacancies. I'll take you there if you follow me." Better than that, she got into my car and the others followed me *à la cavalcade* to Howard Street. Stopping outside Atherton's Hotel, we went in and were introduced to charming Mrs. Atherton who assured us that she was able to take all five of us.

It turned out to be the best digs ever. There was morning tea in bed, hot lunches, afternoon tea and hot suppers after the show. All for just £4 a week. There was a lounge with a record player and stacks of jazz records, including records of some of our favourite bands and musicians. All the time that we were talking to Mrs. Atherton I kept throwing glances at the young lady who had introduced us, only to discover that she was looking at me. I was fast becoming completely infatuated. I think it was love at first sight.

Her name was Margaret (Peggy) and it transpired that she worked in a nearby office. She had been on her way to lunch when we met outside the Alhambra Theatre. On the evening when we moved in to the hotel, Peggy came there to help Rita and her mother as well as to meet the chaps. Both she and Rita were jazz enthusiasts. After our evening meal on would go the records for dancing on the lounge carpet. The more I saw of Peggy, the more I realised that we had much in common – musically, politically, and as far as life in general was concerned. Both Peggy and Rita were active members of the Bradford Rhythm Club. They knew the names of all the important American and British jazz musicians. They were able to recognise the performers on records by their tones and styles, which I thought was an achievement for non-musicians. By the time the week at Atherton's Hotel ended, I was very much in love. After that, all the time we were on tour and whenever we were within driving distance, all roads led, for me, to Bradford.

It was inevitable that I would marry Peggy and we were finally married on October 4th 1938 after my divorce from Annie was finalised. In the meantime, Annie had developed a cancerous growth in the lungs and, as a result of an embolism, she passed away.

Peggy presented me with two more sons, David and Andrew. All four of my sons are close personally to each other, which is an added bonus. Morton lives near me in London and we visit and occasionally go out together. He started life as a drummer but eventually he became an accountant. His twin, Leslie, emigrated to California. He started on trumpet but later he became involved in aircraft design. David lives in Ireland. He went to Trinity College and later became a pianist, a composer and a musical director. Andrew studied piano and art, but became an architect. Now he lives in Scotland, the land of his mother Peggy's forebears. All are happy in their work, which proves that as parents we should let our children have their heads to do their own thing.

Putting on a Show

Continuing touring with Roy Fox led to a week in what was then considered to be a number one theatre venue – the now non-existent Holborn Empire in High Holborn in central London. Obviously, Roy had known about the booking there for a long time but he played his cards close to his chest. Suddenly he wanted us to rehearse an entirely new musical programme and a new comedy routine. Although we had always produced our own comedy numbers (sometimes impromptu) with good effect, he engaged an American husband and wife songwriting team to produce a special number for the show. When we in the band asked him why all this was suddenly happening, the answer was that we were going to play the Holborn Empire.

We were asked to attend a 'rehearsal' to listen to something Mr. and Mrs. Songwriter had prepared for us to perform. She played the piano and together they sang several verses of the most unfunny rubbish it has ever been my misfortune to hear. The end of each verse was punctuated with the comment, "Very Fonny", intended to gain our approval.

We told Roy that it would be a big mistake to perform that number anywhere, let alone in the Holborn Empire. But he insisted that we should do it. We were to memorise it and each of us in turn would have to sing a verse. We would also have to wear comic jackets and wigs. The number duly went into the programme for the Monday night performance. It was delivered with our self-conscious attempts at comedy and met a dead silent audience. It didn't go in the programme for the second house.

Apart from the fact that this particular comic idea was stupid and not at all funny, we had previously always produced our own comedy numbers in the band's shows. We resented the intrusion from outside and thought we were perfectly capable of coming up with ideas of our own. And our ideas usually worked with the audience. We could adapt them until we got them right. For example, one idea arose from the 'Famous Five' having been to see the film *King Kong*. We had been impressed with the sound of the jungle drums and the scene of the natives shouting "Kong!" in homage to the great ape. Maurice Burman suggested that we should use the idea to feature Art Christmas and his ability as a multi-instrumentalist. We talked it over and presented the following idea to Roy. Art would dress up in a gorilla suit. Maurice sitting at his drums on his high rostrum at the back of the stage would beat his tom toms to rhythmic shouts of "Kong!" from the entire band. Behind Maurice there would be a chained gorilla figure struggling to break free. At a certain moment, Art in his gorilla costume would appear to break free of the chains and would lumber ferociously down to the front and glare in a menacing manner at the audience. Then Art the gorilla would turn towards us and pick up and play each instrument in turn.[12] It worked a treat. The performance produced sustained applause and was a tremendous success.

Maybe I should say something more about the shows we did. We would be playing in variety theatres, to seated audiences, as top of the bill. The idea was to give them a complete entertainment, with good music. There would always be one comedy number, but most of the show would be made up of swing pieces, arranged by me, and ballads arranged by Jack Nathan. The swing numbers showed off our jazz soloists, and the ballads would be sung by Denny Dennis or Mary Lee, our Scottish singer. Sometimes there would be a vocal quartet or quintet piece, or Sid Buckman would sing, accompanied by the Cubs and the band. 'Whispering' would be in the programme too. It started out as Roy's signature tune, presented at the beginning just in a few bars to introduce the show. But eventually, after Jack Nathan had written a big, symphonic arrangement around the tune, we used that as a big feature number with various sequences. It would usually come near the finale of the show. Sometimes, after the show, we would have another engagement as well, to play for dancing at another venue.

I always thought it was important to make presenting music an entertainment; to put on a show. It was something that Jack Hylton impressed on us during the time I was with the Metronomes and we had gone to visit him in Southampton. I

---

[12] He could play trumpet and trombone as well as saxes, piano, drums and xylophone (Ed.).

never forgot that lesson and it stood me in good stead all through my career. Hylton used to include one outstanding production number in his show. That idea was one he had picked up from Paul Whiteman. For example, there was a piece Hylton did called 'Somewhere in the Sahara' which actually had camels coming on stage. The audiences loved it. Jack believed in always having something effective to look at.

4.

THE UNION, THE RABIN BAND AND THE BLITZ

All in all, as conditions towards the end of the 1930s changed in various ways, my engagement with Roy was gradually coming to an end. Every year, after the month's unpaid holiday in the summer, we all had to meet the costs at the end of it in equipping ourselves with new uniforms. And in the autumn of 1936, at the beginning of the new season, we were called one by one for an interview with Roy in his dressing room. Now we were informed that we would have to accept a cut of one pound a week. The alternative would be to accept what is known as an 'all-in contract' – an abomination almost like slavery.

Under the normal contract we received a weekly salary to play in theatres. There would be extra pay on top of that for additional work such as recording, broadcasting and playing for dances after the usual show. But an all-in contract meant that although there would be an increase of a couple of pounds a week we would have to perform all the extra work, whatever it might be, for the same money. The basic salary would cover everything.

Ivor Mairants and I refused to take the salary cut or to sign a contract with the new conditions written in to it, but I tried to compromise a little by agreeing to give Roy one free orchestration each month. Eventually, however, and immediately prior to our annual holiday in 1937, we both told

Roy that we would not be returning. So we left the band at the beginning of August that year.[1]

On the last night, each of us received a gold wrist watch engraved with the words, "From Roy and the boys with best wishes". Naturally, Ivor and I were delighted with such an exquisite parting gift, but we were surprised to get anything at all. We remembered what had happened when Peggy Dell, the singer, left because she wanted to return home to Dublin.

After Peggy had given in her notice, the rest of us in the band were called into Roy's dressing room and told that we were not to get a present for her. We were warned that if any of us contributed to a gift for her it would lead to instant dismissal. On her last night at the end of the show, Peggy went to shake hands with Roy. He said to her, "I wish you all the bad luck in the world." A really nasty thing to do, and so unnecessary. It seemed to me that he was becoming a tyrant.

The week before leaving the band, and as a result of the news of my impending departure being printed in the *Melody Maker*, I received a telephone call from Freddy Gardner, the famous alto saxophonist, to tell me that Bert Firman was forming a band to go into the London Casino (now the Prince Edward Theatre) in Old Compton Street and that he would like me to join. The same week a telegram arrived from Jack Payne offering a contract to tour with his orchestra. I had become disenchanted by now with living in digs. I didn't want to go on tour. So I joined Bert Firman's band.[2] Freddy asked if I

[1] The Fox band continued in existence for another year, finally disbanding in August 1938. Fox moved to Australia and then led small bands in New York during the war period. In 1946 he returned to Britain and reformed an orchestra. Soon after, however, he gave up bandleading to run an entertainment agency (Ed.).

[2] Violinist Firman had been leader of the Midnight Follies Orchestra in the 1920s and musical director for Zonophone Records from 1925 to 1928. He later worked in the United States, and with his own bands in Paris, Ostend and Monte Carlo before returning to London in the summer of 1937. The

thought anyone else might be looking for a job with the band and I mentioned Rex Owen, who decided to leave Roy Fox for Firman. When Roy heard that news, he became enraged almost to the point of sacking his entire band. He had, of course, forgotten that a few years before he had taken the brass section from Billy Cotton's band[3] and four musicians (Ivor Mairants, Les Lambert, Jack Nathan and me) from Jack Padbury.

Organising for the Union

I was obsessed with the idea of trying to organise a union, especially when I discovered that cuts were being introduced in all of London's musical establishments. Although I was now back to the situation I had been in at the Café de Paris, earning fifteen pounds weekly with extra for recordings and broadcasts, the Café de Paris was actually now paying twelve to the musicians working there, and pay at the Café Anglais, the Mayfair Hotel and the Embassy Club had been reduced to as little as ten pounds.

I regularly went to Archer Street – the musicians' 'labour exchange' – to investigate the possibility of starting a union for jazz and dance band musicians. At that time the dance band players were considered 'upstarts'. They were really looked down on by the other orchestral and theatre players. In Archer

---

fifteen-piece band he put together for the London Casino was resident there from November 1937 until January 1939. Later in 1939 he moved to the Café de Paris. After the war he led a band in Paris which, for a time, featured Django Reinhardt and Stephane Grappelli, but he then retired from bandleading and worked at the London Metal Exchange until 1976 (Ed.).

[3] Trumpeters Sid Buckman and Nat Gonella, and trombonist Joe Ferrie. This was when Fox put together his band at the Monseigneur club in May 1931 (Ed.).

Street I met Harry Francis, a percussionist who later became Assistant General Secretary of the Musicians' Union. He told me that there was a union already in existence but in the main they were operating for theatre musicians and symphony players. The theatre musicians in general had to be in the union. It was more or less a closed shop for them. The dance band players, however, were still unorganised. All that we needed to do was join the union and help to establish minimum rates of pay for dance band players. But people had to be encouraged to join.

The organisational process started through discussions with musicians who gathered daily in Archer Street, looking for employment. It developed towards mixing with those who had jobs and met after work in Carmen's Café (now the site of a casino), which was also in Archer Street. We decided to begin a 'rank and file' movement known as the Voluntary Organising Committee (VOC), the aim of the VOC being to encourage musicians to join the union. The VOC organised meetings in places where musicians regularly met. Several famous names such as trombonist George Chisholm, trumpeter Tommy McQuater, pianist Pat Dodd and trombonist-arranger Paul Fenhoulet, to name but a few, were regular participants in the meetings the VOC arranged.

Bert Firman and the entire band joined the union. Apart from Firman's, there was a second band at the London Casino. It was led by the conductor Hugo Rignold and was mainly a theatre orchestra performing for the show. The members of that band, as theatre players, were naturally union members, so for the first time the place became a Musicians' Union establishment. I learned that Roy Fox's band was to tour the Mecca dance halls and that rehearsals were in progress at Tottenham Palais. So I decided to go there on an organising mission and succeeded in getting the musicians in the Fox band to join *en bloc*.

At a meeting of the VOC one night, we decided to send a delegation to the Musicians' Union committee. A letter was sent to the Secretary requesting a meeting and, after a week's delay, we were informed that the MU people would allow us to present our ideas. We soon realised, however, when we tried to do so that they weren't interested and we decided to nominate our own members to stand in the next union election. All of our delegates were elected and so a process of reorganising and modernising through the union began. Minimum rates of pay were set for all establishments on the basis of a grading system. This classification directly reflected the then obvious variation in the social class position of the entertainment venues and their clientele. For example, the Café de Paris was graded much higher than, say, Romano's. Bands also elected stewards to make sure that rates and conditions were protected and I became Bert Firman's band steward. Hugo Rignold's band already had a steward in Albert Gordon, the band's pianist, a cheerful little Scot of high integrity.

The theatre of the London Casino was arranged in a similar way, apparently, to the one in the Casino de Paris, in France. The seating for the audience was grouped around tables for use when food and drink was served. There was a dance floor between the area where the diners sat and the stage on which the band played. Steps led down from the tables area to the dance floor, which was also used for the dance routines that formed part of the show. Rignold's band provided the music for the show. Then, when it was over, our band would play for an hour, and afterwards a section of Hugo's band would relieve us for half an hour. Then we would return to play until the end of the proceedings.

Information filtered through that a new show was to be rehearsed and that we would be required to combine with the show band for the overture, *entr'acte* and ballet. Previously, we had only had to play for the finale. That was so that we would be in place and ready to play for dancing immediately the show had ended. The new working arrangement changed the position from the union point of view. I discussed the matter with Albert Gordon and found out from him that the musicians in Hugo Rignold's band were getting a higher rate than we were because of their theatre status and because they played for the show as well as for dancing. Albert suggested that I should try to get the higher rate for our band too. I spoke to Bert Firman about it and he immediately went to the management to discuss the situation. An agreement was reached that we would get the extra money and would also be paid for the additional rehearsals. Everyone was delighted. It also convinced me of the value of unions, and ours in particular.

Eventually, the musicians decided to organise union members into a committee dedicated to raising funds for benevolent purposes; in other words, mainly to help musicians with financial or health difficulties. This became known as the Musicians' Social and Benevolent Council (MSBC). At an initial meeting it was decided to put collecting boxes in all venues where musicians performed. It was also suggested that golf-playing musicians might get together to organise a section to play tournaments from which money for benevolent purposes could be raised. The MSBC received enthusiastic support and suggestions poured in from all directions. The best of these suggestions eventually was the famous annual Jazz Jamboree from the end of the 1930s. The idea was to hire a theatre and get the bandleaders to agree to donate their bands' services for the event so that all the proceeds could go towards the MSBC's purposes. 'Jazz Jamboree' was often something of a misnomer, because mainly dance bands played, instilling a bit of swing into their programme for the occasion. The money raised from all these various activities and collections was banked in an interest-bearing account from which the MSBC could allocate a sum of money to the Musicians' Union London District Benevolent Fund, and disburse small sums to sick or needy musicians.

During the time I was involved with the VOC and an activist for the Central London branch of the Musicians' Union, there was a dispute between the Union and the management of the Prince of Wales Theatre in Coventry Street. A new musical was about to start there but we learned that the musicians engaged for the show were not MU members and were not going to be paid the union rate. We tried to negotiate with the management but they refused to meet us. So members were told a strike was imminent. A team of pickets (including yours truly) was organised with instructions to picket the theatre entrance with leaflets and posters to tell the public of the dispute.

We had to be careful not to break the law by approaching members of the public or standing still (causing an obstruction). It was necessary to keep moving or be arrested. The Musicians' Union bought some seats for the opening night performance so that activists could attend and create a disturbance. During the show one of the actors had to deliver the line, "What shall we do?" When he did so, one of our colleagues in the audience stood up and shouted in reply, as though it had been rehearsed, "Pay the musicians their proper fee." A little later, Jack Davis, a bass player, walked across the balcony from where he had been seated to a point where he could climb down on to the stage. He did so, walked to the front centre of the stage and gave a speech about the poor rates of pay. Of course, the police removed him and arrested him. But the result was that the management met us to settle the dispute and we demanded that musicians employed in the show should to be members of the union. It was a great victory.

Oscar Rabin

I'll mention in passing something that happened during the time I was with Bert Firman. A saxophone teacher named Henry Nichols, who was also a bachelor of science, had the idea of arranging a series of X-rays of saxophone players' embouchures (in other words, their way of applying their lips, teeth and tongue in playing wind instruments). He arranged to publish the results in *Rhythm*, a music magazine on sale at the time (1938). The idea was that the X-ray photographs would enable readers to compare the differences between players' methods of blowing. It was an interesting idea because the shape of the teeth and of the palate and the roof of the mouth, all in combination with the mouthpiece and the way it is blown, certainly influences the distinctiveness of the sound. So I agreed to take part. One of the other musicians involved was a tenor sax player named Benny Greenwood. Mr. Nichols remarked that Benny's embouchure was remarkably like mine. I wasn't surprised, however, seeing that Benny had been a pupil of mine. I did a bit of tutoring over the years, though not a lot. In fact I turned a lot of people down who wanted tuition from me.

A week before New Year's Eve 1938, the end of show notice went on the notice board at the London Casino, which meant that we would be out of work the following week. Although this was the beginning of six months' unemployment, as far as a regular playing job was concerned, I was able to get work arranging for the BBC orchestrations department. A year previously on some Sunday concert gigs, I had met Wally Wallond, who was a pianist and the manager of the department, and also the double bass player Peter Akister, a wonderful arranger, who wrote arrangements for the BBC. So those contacts helped. It was also through Wally that I met the pianist Norrie Paramor, who would later work with me regularly in my own band and become my partner.

After a while things began to look up again as far as possibilities for playing were concerned. I had a phone call from Billy Bisset, a Canadian bandleader working in London, who offered me an engagement at the Café Anglais. He said, "We're having a rehearsal on Monday morning at eleven o'clock. Can you make it?" I said I'd be there, and on the Monday morning I arrived in good time to unpack my instruments. While I was doing so I noticed two other tenor players standing in a corner. I played for about an hour with the band and then Bisset said to me, "That's all. Please phone me tomorrow morning." He told me that the money would be fifteen pounds a week. I realised that it wasn't a rehearsal but an audition and I went away feeling very angry, because by then I was well known and my auditioning days were over.

When I got home I had a call from Oscar Rabin to ask me if I would like to go in to the Hammersmith Palais to play second alto sax in his band. He told me, "The job entails seven afternoons and seven evenings and the money is eight pounds a week." I told him that I was not playing alto any more, but that I could play the parts he needed on tenor sax. "If you are prepared to accept that, I'll come along." He agreed and told me, "We start at three o'clock for an hour, and then back again at four thirty for another hour. I'll give you the rest of the information when I see you there." So I joined Oscar Rabin. I had decided not to take the Café Anglais job with Billy Bisset because of his dishonesty. He called me and asked why I hadn't telephoned him as he had requested and I told him that I was starting another job. I stayed with Oscar from the spring of 1939 until the end of 1942.[4]

---

[4] Born in Latvia in 1899, Oscar Rabin came to Britain as a child. He originally studied violin but later specialised on bass sax. Rabin led the Romany Band at Wimbledon Palais in 1926-8, and then held long residences

I had heard rumours that the band was co-operative and I was particularly interested in being involved in such an organisation. I mentioned the rumours I had heard to Oscar and he didn't deny them. But he said, "Let's see how we get on. You might not like it, but I'll review the situation later if you stay." I started to write some arrangements for the band's broadcasts and Oscar thought they made the band sound better. So I began to write for him regularly.[5]

The band consisted of three saxes (all doubling clarinet) – Johnny Swinfen, lead alto, and myself and Sid Brown, tenor saxes; three brass – Tommy Balderson and Bobby 'Bix' Benstead, trumpets, and Hamish Christie, trombone; Alf Caplan, piano; Harry Davis, guitar and compere; Gary Gowan, bass and vocals; Cecil Laley-Walden, drums; and, of course, Oscar, on violin and bass sax. I thought that the sound of the band would be greatly improved by adding a trombone and another sax. I broached the matter with Oscar and, after some thought, he augmented the band in the way I had suggested. Tony Thorpe was added as the second trombonist, but he became a soloist with the band because he was a very superior player. The additional saxophonist was Harry Conn.

In spite of the long hours, working with Oscar's band was becoming enjoyable. The chaps were friendly and kind. Oscar had an excellent sense of humour and could be very funny in the bandroom. One day I suggested that he should try his comedy on stage. He went white with fear. "No," he said, "I'd be too frightened." The matter was never mentioned again. Apart from making records and doing broadcasts, which

---

at various London venues including the Astoria. From 1935 to 1940 (apart from the break mentioned later in the text) his band was resident at the Hammersmith Palais. It also recorded and broadcast from 1935 (Ed.).

[5] Albert McCarthy, who heard the band in the early 1940s, writes (in his *The Dance Band Era*) that "at this time it was following a more adventurous musical policy than it had done in the past..." (Ed.).

helped the finances, the band occasionally played for Jewish weddings, which were very well paid. So things were looking up. Then, on September 3rd 1939 the Second World War started and, in a state of panic, the Government decreed that all entertainment halls should close. So, for the moment, we lost the Hammersmith Palais job on which the band depended for its existence.

The Phoney War

I couldn't afford to be out of work. I heard that the officials at Hammersmith Town Hall were engaging men to dig trenches and to set up protection screens for the windows of what were considered important buildings. Of course, this was in preparation for the air raids that were expected. So Oscar's son Bernard and I went to the Town Hall and joined a queue of men all intent on getting a job. There was work for everyone, and Bernard and I were employed to carry sandbags to a location at a convent in Hammersmith Road.

While we were waiting to be interviewed for work I had noticed a navvy trundling a wheelbarrow at a very leisurely pace. On it were three sandbags. I mentally criticised the tortoise-like gait and thought, "I'll show them how it should be done." But I learned some lessons quickly. The first was not to try to work like a musician, in a white shirt, collar and tie. The tie came off after two minutes. The second lesson was a reminder that even in labouring there is a union position to take into account. From the pile of filled sandbags each labourer had to lift a bag on to his shoulder and walk with it about a hundred yards. The bag had to be deposited near some other men whose job was to stack the bags side by side and layer on layer in front of the windows. I tried to show how I could work by running with the bags twice as fast as everyone else. Eventually one of the men passing me said out of the corner of his mouth, "What the fuck do you think you're doing?" Instant conformity became necessary.

The work was arduous and long. We started at 7.00 a.m., stopped at 8.30 for breakfast (which everyone brought in boxed packages) and started again after twenty minutes. When a pub nearby opened we were allowed to go for a pint – one at a time. There was a break for lunch at 1.00 p.m., on again at two until tea at five, and then on again until 7.00 p.m. It was twelve hours of hard graft and then home, tired to the point of exhaustion and filthy. My white shirt was unrecognisably black and I was ready to eat a horse by the time the day was finished. Then I just wanted to get to bed as soon as possible. I slept like an innocent child, solidly for eight untroubled hours.

The foreman visited the various work locations. He would watch the workforce in action while picking his fingernails with a penknife, wearing a straw hat and leaning against a wall, alongside which he had propped his bike. I am sure he was ill-disposed towards Bernard and me because he knew that we weren't labourers. He arrived one morning and shouted what sounded like, "Who's got a used card?" He meant 'youth's card'. He was checking up whether anyone who had been signed on for the job was too young to be doing it. He must have thought I was the one with the youth's card because Bernard was tall, big built and looked much older than his years. When Bernard owned up the foreman told him to go to the office, collect any pay owing to him and leave.

A couple of days later he told me to load a long, low-built lorry with sandbags. They were wet and consequently heavier than usual. He stood watching me and waiting for me to give up. But I knew that if I failed I would get my cards. The vehicle platform was about the height of my chest. But, as layer after layer of sandbags reached the height of my head, it was obvious that they would soon be too high for me to reach and that was what he was anticipating. What he didn't know was that I had done a considerable amount of weight lifting. I hoisted the bags to my shoulder as if I was lifting weights and, using that method, I could throw them on to the lorry. When the task was done, I turned to the foreman with thumbs up and went back to the previous job moving loads of sandbags by wheelbarrow.

I learned another lesson with the wheelbarrow. Remembering the navvy with the three sandbags and thinking I could do much better, I asked Bernard to fill the barrow with as many bags as it would hold. But when I grabbed the handles to lift the barrow's legs I couldn't move them. "OK, Bernard, take one off," I said. He did, and I still failed to lift the barrow. This was repeated over and over until – as you've guessed – there were just three bags left!

Eventually a message came that Hammersmith Palais was re-opening. I said goodbye to my colleagues. They had become close friends and were, in my opinion, the salt of the earth. I collected my card and wages and went back to working in music.

On the band's return to the Palais, we were told that it was not known what business would be like so Claude Langdon, the owner, was only prepared to pay each of the musicians five pounds per week. I had been making over eight pounds shifting sandbags at the convent so I thought that offering five was a cheek. Apart from that, the minimum union minimum rate was seven pounds. I was asked to report the matter to the branch secretary. The union organiser called to discuss the situation. Before he left he told us that it had been agreed that temporarily we would be paid the union minimum. It soon became apparent, however, that business was booming and not long afterwards we were paid ten pounds a week.

It was the period of the 'phoney war'. There were troops everywhere and it was as if everyone was waiting for the fighting really to begin. But, for the moment a lot of people were looking for entertainment, maybe to take their minds off the future. Each session was a full house with every kind of uniform in evidence. It was clear that an increase in pay would not be forthcoming without some pressure being arranged. Oscar was approached and asked to do the 'necessary' with the Palais management. When it was pointed out to him that it was to his advantage, he had a meeting with Mr. Langdon and was able to report back that we would all be getting an increase of three pounds a week. "Ask and ye shall receive...."

When the bombing began, Peggy and I were renting a flat in Hammersmith Grove close to the Palais, so that I could avoid having to travel in an air raid.[6] After a while, the night bombing became continuous and the management proposed that the musicians in the band should stay at the Palais until the raids ended in the morning. We were provided with a room filled with camp beds. Some years later I was contracted to play in the Palais with the Pieces of Eight, as the relief band for Joe Loss, and the bandroom we used was the room in which I and the other Rabin musicians had slept during the air raids. I discovered then that there was merely a thin flat roof overhead and a glass partition covered with a wooden panel facing the street. If a bomb had fallen nearby none of us would have survived. It was just the shared comfort of a close human relationship bonding us together that made us feel safe.

[6] "From 7 September until 3 November 1940 London was attacked every night but one; thereafter, apart from a lull in February 1941, raids were regular until 16 May, when Hitler withdrew the Luftwaffe for service on the Russian front.... Altogether about 20,000 died and another 25,000 were hurt in the London blitz between September 1940 and May 1941" (R. Gray, *A History of London*, 1978). Bombing largely ceased after May 16th 1941 until the V1 and V2 rocket attacks of 1944-5 (Ed.).

Dodging the Bombs

Oscar couldn't stand the nightly bombing. It was shattering his nerves. So he decided to take the band out of London, on tour to play in provincial variety theatres and dance halls. He was aware of my extensive previous experience of touring with Roy Fox and asked me what I thought of the project. I said that I thought it could be successful provided that our shows included comedy. I told him to concentrate on entertainment. I said, "You need to bear in mind that seated audiences are completely different from those in dance halls." He got the message, so once again Peggy and I hit the road in a coach.

It was then, while we were on tour, that I came up with the idea of persuading Oscar to have a band within the band. I said to him, "If you were to have a couple of numbers with a dixieland style in the show, it would help to make it interesting. I could single out the players who are capable of playing in that style and arrange the music to make it sound right." He liked the idea and told me to go ahead. But then I remembered what Roy Fox had done. After Ivor Mairants and I left Roy in August 1937, he had used our name 'the Cubs' for a vocal trio that replaced the one we had had in his band. I didn't want something like that to happen again. I said to Oscar, "By the way, I hope you don't mind, but I would like my name to be connected with the small band." He agreed immediately without a demur.

That week we were playing in the Glasgow Empire and were staying with Peggy's sister and her husband out at Croftfoot on the south side. When I arrived back there after the show one night, I told them that I had the chance to start a band as part of Oscar's show. I said, "I need some suggestions for a band name that will fit with the name 'Gold'. I'd like something along the lines of 'Red Nichols and his Five Pennies'. Harry Gold and his...?" So we sat up for a couple of hours sharing thoughts. We played around with the names 'Diggers', 'Miners', 'Nuggets' and 'Panners', but none of them seemed quite right. Then Peggy's brother-in-law jokingly said, "Why not 'Pieces of Eight'?" I said, "That's exactly the idea." So the next day I told Oscar that the name of the band would be 'Harry Gold and his Pieces of Eight'. That's how it was born.

The musicians I put together for my band were the cornet player 'Bix' Benstead (who later went to Canada and played in the Mounties Band), clarinettist Harry Conn and trombone player Tony Thorpe, all excellent musicians for the style I wanted.[7] Of course, there wasn't an alternative for the rhythm section. Eddie Palmer was the pianist, Bill Whinnie was on bass – both new recruits since the Hammersmith Palais days – and Cecil Laley-Walden was the drummer.

I mentioned earlier that the Rabin band had the reputation of being a co-operative organisation and that I had asked Oscar about the possibility of being part of the co-operative. He had put me off at the time. I felt that I was a candidate for inclusion, but it soon became apparent that there was no foundation for that belief. I came to realise that what had been thought of as a co-operative was merely a partnership between the original members of the old Romany band – the band that Oscar had led at the Wimbledon Palais in the 1920s. One by one they were being got rid of. The first victim was pianist Alf Caplan. While we were working at Hammersmith Palais, Oscar decided that he wanted a better pianist. But how do you dispense with a partner with whom you have been connected for many years? Easy. You make him the leader of another

---

[7] Bobby Benstead had joined Rabin in April 1938. Apart from his period of war service he was with the band until the early 1950s. Later he played in the London Palladium Orchestra and then emigrated to Canada. He died suddenly in 1960 aged only 38. Tony Thorpe, a Canadian, had worked with Ambrose and Henry Hall and freelanced extensively. In the 1960s he played bass trombone in the Royal Opera House Orchestra (Ed.).

band – in this case the relief band at the Palais. When the relief band gets the sack, so does the ex-partner. In the meantime, engage another pianist. Admittedly, the replacement was a great improvement in the person of Norman Stenfalt,[8] but the episode left a nasty taste.

Soon after touring started, Sid Brown left and was replaced by George Roberts, who had arrived from the West Indies with Ken Johnson. George was a survivor of the bomb explosion which hit the Café de Paris during the war.[9] He was a fine sax player and was also an electronics engineer with a science degree. He, Peggy and I often stayed in the same digs. One evening he called us into his room to demonstrate a record player with an automatic record changer that he had made. Above the turntable were ten records he had stacked. The motor was started up and after the first record ended a second one dropped with some clicks on to the table. At the same time the other eight records started to fly off in different directions amid peals of laughter from the three of us. I told George to stick to music.

Harry Conn had been playing second alto to Johnny Swinfen, but Johnny left to start a nightclub in Brighton. Harry was moved to lead and a sixteen year old youth named Wally Stott came in on second alto to complete a lovely sax section. All of these various departures were manipulated quite subtly – the

[8] Stenfalt worked with the band while it was at the Hammersmith Palais but he left it when Rabin began touring and was replaced by Eddie Palmer. Stenfalt worked with Nat Gonella, Johnny Claes and Frank Weir, before being called up for war service in 1941. He later became a notable modern jazz pianist. According to Harry, Stenfalt's style showed 'modern' tendencies while he was with the Rabin band (Ed.).

[9] Ken 'Snake Hips' Johnson, born in Guyana (then British Guiana), worked in England as a tap-dancer, toured the West Indies, and returned to Britain in 1936, becoming leader of the Jamaica Emperors band, which began a residency at the Café de Paris in late 1939. While working there he was killed by a bomb during an air raid on March 8th 1941 (Ed.)

final one being that of trombonist Hamish Christie – and gradually the co-operative myth of the band was laid bare. What it came down to finally was a straightforward partnership between Oscar and Harry Davis.[10] I have the feeling that the latter was the source of the whole manoeuvre.

Still, we had lots of fun with the Rabin band and I always found Oscar to be an enthusiastic participant, although he was constantly nervous of bombing. Unfortunately, we experienced all the blitzes that hit the provincial towns, apart from Coventry. Birmingham, Liverpool, Manchester, Plymouth, Swansea and Glasgow were just some of the towns that were bombed while we were there. One Sunday evening concert we played was in a cinema at Pendleton on the outskirts of Manchester. An air raid warning sounded just as the show was about to begin and Oscar's expression became grim. Although the colour of his face had changed to a chalky white, he put on an air of bravado and looked at me with a grim smile as if to say, "Here they are again. We can't avoid it so carry on." We finished the show and then the police announced that nobody was to leave the cinema until they gave permission. We had started to pack up our instruments when a bomb dropped on two houses near the stage door. Oscar and Ken Beaumont, the guitarist-singer, had gone into their shared dressing room by then and fragments of brickwork were blasted across their room by the explosion. Oscar and Ken were injured seriously enough to justify their removal to hospital, where they remained for three days. In the meantime the show went on without them.

The roof of the vehicle that had brought our instruments had been blown clean off. As we musicians in the band were in digs in the centre of Manchester we decided to travel on the

[10] The friendship of Rabin and Davis dated from 1924, and their band had its first engagement at the Palace Hotel, Southend in 1925. Subsequently it was billed as 'Oscar Rabin and his Romany Band with Harry Davis' (Ed.).

roofless lorry, taking what luggage and instruments we could load on to it. It was a nightmare journey. There were fires everywhere. As we got nearer to the city we were driven over firehoses strewn across roads while the firemen were doing their best to put the flames out. The van was fully loaded with our goods and people, so I elected to sit with my legs dangling over the tailboard so that I could see everything that was going on. The van driver decided to drive first to his home to check that his wife and child were still alive. On arrival, he went inside the house and brought his family out, sitting them at his side in the vehicle, and then we drove on. After the lorry had moved about fifty yards, three bombs fell, one after the other, in the centre of the road. I saw the first of them explode and yelled "Duck!" – which, of course, I did. That first bomb destroyed the driver's home. Wasn't it lucky he decided to pick his family up?

Each of us was dropped somewhere close to our respective digs, and when Peggy and I alighted from the lorry I carried my tenor sax while she carried a small case with nightclothes. The rest of our things had been left in the cinema. As we moved away from the lorry in the darkness, bombs began to fall again and anti-aircraft guns retaliated. As we wended our way towards our digs in the Oxford Road, I lifted the tenor sax case over our heads for protection. In retrospect, it seems a very pointless action. Anything that might have fallen on top of the case would have gone straight through.

Oscar and Ken Beaumont returned with minor scars. Oscar's first words on rejoining us were, "That bastard Hitler is out to get me. He's after all the Jews." A little over the top, I thought. Anyway, the Rabin band was doing very well in its travels around the country and its popularity was continually growing.

Green's Playhouse

Occasionally we would have a period of relaxation, for example when we played a month's residency in the famous Green's Playhouse in Glasgow. That was a place where most of the well-known big bands performed. Joe Loss always played there twice a year, attracting record attendances. He worked for a percentage of the box office takings. His record there was finally broken by the appearance of a comedy dance band known as Doctor Crock and his Crackpots. Dr. Crock was the pseudonym of a fine clarinettist named Harry Hines. At that time he was also Chairman of the Musicians' Social and Benevolent Council.

The two Green brothers who ran the Playhouse were originally from a family of circus people. They had a sharp eye for business. Once, Joe Loss asked Fred Green if he would get another clock to replace the one on the wall opposite the bandstand where the visiting band always played. Joe was fed up because the clock never told the right time and he could never know when to finish his set and hand over to the resident band. When the large hand of the clock had passed the twelve it would gather speed running downhill towards the six, gaining at least ten minutes on the way. On the climb back to the hour position it would slow to snail's pace, like a tired cyclist struggling to the top of the hill. Arriving, as it were, at the hilltop it would pause for breath for a minute to get ready for the downhill run to half past the hour. But when Joe pleaded for a replacement clock, Mr. Green simply said, "Mr. Loss, If I put another clock in, will it bring in any more people?" The old clock stayed. The Playhouse was a grand place. It consisted of a huge cinema and a dance floor, seven floors up, which could accommodate about 4,000 people. It doesn't exist now, but it was wonderful then to see that vast dance floor full of couples dancing the ballroom dance styles in stately fashion and then erupting into an almost frantic physical display for a set of the new 'jive' sessions. Rock and roll dances today are tame by comparison.

Glasgow is a lovely city populated with friendly, generous people, kindly to a fault. But, as everywhere else, there were some who were ready to upset the apple cart. Occasionally a fight might break out between rival gangs. During one of our sessions, some members of a gang walked right across our bandstand, pushing us aside to get to a rival group already on the dance floor. They were intent on starting a rumpus. Of course, it didn't take long for all the resident heavies to join in. Oh, what fun!

The Greens knew how to handle any disturbance. During the war, some goods were scarce including cigarettes and whisky. On one occasion, Fred, the elder of the brothers, was standing by the kiosk on the balcony of the Playhouse. A system of rationing was operating for sales there. A customer asked the sales lady for a packet of Players' cigarettes. When she replied that there were none, the customer started to get aggressive. Mr. Green intervened saying, "It's no use carrying on like that. She said there were no cigarettes available." That provoked the response, "What's it to you? Who the hell do you think you are?" Fred Green said to the sales lady, "Give me a packet," at which she reached below the counter and produced one. Holding the packet up, Fred said, "That's who I am and if you're not careful, you'll be going down the hard way."

One afternoon, arriving at the Playhouse balcony just before one of our sessions was due to start, I was surprised to see two large travelling trunks outside Oscar's dressing room. They were obviously too big to get through the door. He was standing there proudly admiring them. "Harry, my boy," he said, "What do you think of those?" Well, during the war it was virtually impossible to obtain articles of the quality and rarity of those trunks, and delivered straight to your front door, you might say. I congratulated him on acquiring such superb commodities and then moved on to the band's dressing room to get ready for the session.

At the end of the afternoon performance, as I was on my way to my evening meal, I asked Oscar how he had managed to obtain such envied goods. With a certain amount of modesty he said, "I was lucky. The manager told me they were available and, of course, as they had fallen off a lorry they were cheap." When I arrived back for the evening performance, I noticed that the trunks had gone. Oscar was livid. "Someone took them away while the hall was empty," he explained. "If they're not back by the morning, I'm going to the police." Lo and behold, the following morning found the two trunks once again outside Oscar's dressing room.

Of course, we all knew that the manager was behind the operation. He was well in with the Glaswegian criminal fraternity. Probably he had been responsible not only for supplying the trunks to Oscar in the first place but for their disappearance later. In that connection, I was told that all of the big bandleaders had to pay protection money to the Glasgow crime bosses to keep the peace, as it were. It seems that fracas like the one I mentioned earlier could take place if the payments were not forthcoming. It was like Chicago during Prohibition, in some respects.

After Glasgow we went on to Liverpool. Peggy and I had rented a sitting room and bedroom for the week on the top floor of a tenement block. There were two nights of the usual air raids while we were there, but we decided it wasn't worth getting up during the bombing. If we were hit, too bad. On the second night, however, Peggy said, "There's something moving in the bed." "You're imagining it. Go to sleep," I said. But the words were no sooner out than I felt a movement, so I got out. I could see a raised lump moving under the blanket. I grabbed the lump and slowly moved the blanket aside to reveal a mouse. I thought, "What shall I do with it?" Then an idea: "Throw it into the street." I couldn't touch it with my bare hand, so I picked the frightened animal up in a piece of paper and threw it out of the open window. Or so I thought. My hand came back with the mouse still there. I just hadn't got the heart, though it seemed necessary. After four attempts I let go successfully, but sleep eluded us after that.

Whenever we returned to London we stayed at the Bonnington Hotel in Southampton Row. Because it is a fairly high building, we felt relatively safe. It had an air raid shelter below ground and it was cheap at one pound a night.

Putting Down Roots

While we were in the Holborn area of London, I suggested to Peggy that it might be good to look for somewhere to make a permanent home. She agreed and, walking along Theobalds Road, I saw a notice 'Flat to let. Ring bell Flat 6'. A kindly, middle-aged lady answered when I rang and told me I needed to "go to the city and meet the trustee and negotiate with him." When I found him and we discussed terms in a nearby hostelry I realised he was more anxious to do a deal than I was. People were leaving London in droves and there were empty flats and houses everywhere.

I signed an agreement on a twelve monthly basis, with options to renew, at the inexpensive rent of nineteen shillings and sixpence – just under a pound a week. It was a large flat with a bedroom, bathroom/toilet, lounge, and kitchen/dining room. We moved in the following week. Our furniture had been stored in the house in Hammersmith Grove near the Palais and I got Oscar's touring manager to help with a van for the move. Right next door to the front door to the flats was a pub, The Yorkshire Grey. It struck me that the pub would be very useful after getting our gear up two flights of stairs.

After the bedroom was ship-shape and the kitchen ready for operation, I went next door to quench my thirst. In fact I was the only customer. At the bar the huge barman asked, "Good morning sir, what would you be having?" This elicited the reply, "A large Powers Gold Label (whiskey) and a pint of Guinness." He brought the liquor for me, and a glass for himself, commenting, "That would be a good Dublin drink." When I asked how much I owed he said, "That's on the house, sir." A nice Irish welcome to my new neighbourhood, I thought. I felt at home. Some time later, my band, the Pieces of Eight, played at the Yorkshire Grey every Sunday evening.

The touring schedule with the Rabin band continued. We revisited many of the towns we had played at previously but now we mostly played at theatres, rather than the dance halls. I always enjoyed working at the theatres because it meant that we could see the acts on the same bill with our band. Beyond that, there was an additional entertainment perk on tour. Because of a custom accepted by cinema managers in every town, at the time, we could see films in the afternoon just by presenting our professional cards as musicians at the cinema box offices. That practice seems to been stopped, but I've never understood why. Usually there are plenty of seats available during matinée performances, so allowing free admission can't affect the takings.

While we were still on the road, Oscar was engaged by the BBC for the band to broadcast from a studio in Bristol for a radio show to be called 'Band of the Week'. I'm not sure whether the idea was instigated by the Government or whether it came just from the BBC. But the intention was that there should be a radio dance band show provided by a different band each week and designed to maintain public morale. The show, broadcast once a week, would feature the 'band of the week' and several artistes and a comedian. Bristol was chosen as the broadcasting location because it seemed to be out of the dangerous bombing zone.

Ours was the first band chosen for the series. Oscar celebrated by acquiring a new instrument for Eddie Palmer, our pianist, to use on pretty tunes. It was called a novachord and was a kind of electronic organ, quite different from present day keyboards. The keys were laid out as on an organ in three tiers. The instrument had several stops or switches that produced an enormous variety of tone colours. There was one problem. It was very heavy. The studio from which we were to broadcast was at the top of a staircase in a church hall hired for the occasion by the BBC. So there was no staff to move the novachord. We took it in turns to heave the monster up the stairs. Oscar was told firmly that we weren't prepared to take it down again.

The producer for the show was a man from Birmingham named Philip Brown, a well-known broadcasting bandleader who was also a lyricist. When we arrived on the first day, he was looking for some songwriting co-operation and asked me if I would write a melody to fit the words he had written for the programme's signature tune. I was happy to co-operate. It meant that every week for as long as bands visited Bristol, the signature tune would be played, and my royalties would increase as a result.

We kept on touring until one day I decided that we should get a place to live near Bristol. The main idea was to have somewhere where Peggy could be safe away from the bombing. We found some rooms in Weston-Super-Mare, which was attractive because of the seaside setting and because, with our touring schedules and the Bristol radio broadcasts, I could get back there frequently. We were joined there by Benny Keen (one of the sax players) and his wife. It was just as well we made the arrangements then, because

Peggy and Benny's wife both became pregnant, which meant an almost permanent residence for them there. Benny and I went to Weston as often as possible, but in the meantime the touring continued, with the band mainly playing theatres.

Eventually, while we were playing another week in Glasgow, I received a letter from HM Government requesting my appearance for a medical examination at an office in Sauchiehall Street. I thought, "This is the end of my playing in a band for a while." I was certain I would be called up for one of the armed services, as I knew I was healthy and fit. I went at the appointed time. An eye specialist asked me how my eyesight was, which surprised me as I thought it was his job to find out. But I had no intention of pulling any fast ones and told him, "Fine with the glasses." The eye test which followed graded me A2. Then there was a chest examination, with the chest doctor rounding it off by giving me one hell of a thump on my back and saying, "Good man, you're A1." I could have told him that. Next, the stomach specialist, and again the questions: "Any past trouble?" "No." "Are you well?" "Yes, thank you, very well." A few prods here and there and then, "Get up on to the couch." All medical couches are made for giants, as far as I'm concerned, so it was a climb a mile high. "On your back," was the order, and I thought, "Ah, an opportunity for a quick doze." No chance! He was about to examine me, stopped short and exclaimed, "You've got bad feet!" Well, I knew that, but I didn't think saying it would cut any ice. He didn't bother to examine my stomach but told me to stand up. Then exercises. "On your toes, knees bend" etc. I had to wait while he brought in two more doctors. I went through the paces again (almost like an audition) and was told to get dressed and go to a table to collect a card.

I told the man at the table, "I'd like to apply for a deferral of call-up as I have a contract that will expire in a month or two." He replied, "Deferral? We don't want you!" I couldn't believe it! I went out, walking in a dream for a couple of hundred yards, not knowing where I was going. Suddenly I found myself outside a pub. I went in and ordered a Scotch (I didn't dare ask for Irish whiskey in Glasgow!) and a pint of 'heavy'. I downed them both in one go and re-ordered. Drinking at a much slower pace, I stood at the bar trying to understand why I'd been rejected. But I couldn't, especially because my youngest brother Laurie had been accepted even though he had only one eye.

I phoned Weston-Super-Mare to give Peggy the news, only to discover that she had been admitted to the maternity ward in hospital. Having been given the phone number and asked the hospital receptionist what was happening I was told I had another son. Soon after, the band was engaged to play again for the BBC 'Band of the Week' programme in Bristol. So I was able to go to Weston and see Peggy and the new addition to the family, whom we called David.

It was while the band was waiting for the red light to go on in the Bristol studio for a broadcast that I heard that my brother Sid had been killed on active service in the Middle East. A telegram had been phoned through to the studio with that simple message. Oscar, with a great deal of sympathetic understanding, sent someone to get me a large brandy. I'm not sure how I got through that broadcast without breaking down, but the concentration on the job in hand helped considerably.

It was only much later that the news of how Sid had died came through. In fact, I first heard about it in a most strange way that convinced me, after many years of joking about the matter, of the value of spiritualism. One day I was with a number of other musicians in Harry Conn's flat. Someone claimed to be a spiritualist medium and I challenged him to conduct a seance. He was very reluctant and the whole affair was conducted in an atmosphere of much vocal disbelief from me and others present. But at some point, after various strange occurrences, a voice with a Chinese accent suddenly came from the medium's mouth, saying, "There is someone I must bring through from our side. It is important for the one called Harry." Then there was another voice calling my name. I still thought it was a fake but the others urged me to answer, so I did. The voice claimed to be my brother and said, "At last. Oh, my head, my shoulder, my arms and legs. The heat is awful." I asked, "What happened?" He replied, "We were sitting there and suddenly..." As he said that last word there was the sense of an explosion which we all agreed was felt by everyone present. The chuckles stopped and I asked, "How many?" "Eight" was the reply and the voice started to give the names.

Six months later an official report from the War Office about Sid's death was finally received. It said, "He was sitting with his comrades outside a cafe on Christmas Day when someone threw a hand grenade. He died with multiple injuries to head, shoulder and other parts of his body. He is buried with seven of his comrades in the Lebanon." That verified beyond all doubt what took place at the seance that evening. I am now a convinced spiritualist.

The war situation was about to change in favour of the Allied forces in Africa and Italy. Landings would soon be made on the European continent (starting from Sicily in July 1943) and the daily and all-night bombing had virtually ceased, which meant that we could return to our flat in Holborn. Our neighbours there, Mrs. Bedford and her daughter Mary who lived in Flat 6, were charmed by Peggy and young David, now six months old. There hadn't been young people in the building for a long time and they took to us as though we were family.

I had to leave London again for a time – taking Peggy and David with me – because Oscar had another month's engagement at Green's in Glasgow, but I decided that I would give my notice to leave the band at the end of that month.

While we were at the Playhouse, the resident band's union steward told me that they were going on strike. They were joining with all Glasgow musicians in strike action for more money. He asked me, "What will your lot do?" That was a real poser. None of us in the band would be prepared to 'blackleg'. But we weren't employed by the Green brothers. Our contract was with Oscar. I told the steward I would get Oscar's reaction and let him know.

I told Oscar what was about to happen and suggested that he should imply to the Green brothers that our band was likely to support the other musicians. "Say that you don't agree with the strike but that you can't stop us if we join the strike action."

In the meantime the union's Scottish organiser Jimmy MacBean called a meeting in the union office in West Nile Street. I was invited to attend as Oscar's band steward. It seemed that the Glasgow musicians were grossly underpaid and the employers would not meet the union officials and were not prepared to talk. At the meeting Jimmy MacBean explained that the Emergency Powers Act prohibited strikes during wartime.

I pointed out that there need not be a strike. All that the musicians needed to do was to exercise their right to give notice of withdrawing their labour. If, by some strange chance, everyone gave notice at the same time, it would be unfortunate for the employers but it would not be a strike. It proved to be the correct tactic. Within three days, the employers asked to meet the union officials and there was no strike. The upshot was that the Glasgow musicians elected me to attend the meeting with the employers on their behalf.

During the meeting, Mr. Green said to me, "Mr. Gold, yer cannae expect these musicians to get the same as yersel'" Knowing that he was a very religious man, I quoted the parable of the vineyards to him, reminding him that the labourer is worthy of his hire. Agreement was finally reached, giving pay increases and obtaining union recognition.

Eventually, it was back to London, for me to find work.

5.

AMBROSE, GERALDO AND A BAND OF MY OWN

After the time with Oscar, I worked occasionally with other big bands. I was with Geraldo[1] for several months in 1943, but it was not a matter of non-stop touring, as with Oscar, but mainly broadcasting and working in the studios. I've often been asked by interviewers if I have enjoyed my life in the music profession and my reply has always been "Yes". But, on reflection, that isn't completely true. Mostly I've enjoyed myself immensely, but with Geraldo's orchestra I didn't. It was not that I disliked the music we played or the quality of the performers. It was a lovely band to play in, musically. But, for some reason, I got the 'cold shoulder' from the other musicians in the band, apart from the ones who were my old mates. Nobody spoke to me during our breaks when we were socialising. Apart from that, I didn't have the chance to solo and yet I was, by then, well-known as a soloist. The other

[1] Geraldo's orchestra, according to Albert McCarthy in *The Dance Band Era*, was "in many ways the band that dominated the '40s in Britain." Born in London in 1904, Gerald Bright studied at the Royal Academy of Music and, in the 1920s, fronted dance bands in England and on the Continent. Influenced by a visit to Latin America, he formed his 'Gaucho Tango Band' early in the 1930s and adopted the stage name Geraldo, which he kept for the rest of his career as a bandleader. After the break-up of the tango band, his dance orchestra (which he had led alongside it) became outstanding partly through personnel changes in the late 1930s, especially the hiring of saxophonists Harry Hayes, Andy McDevitt and George Evans, all of whom were good jazz soloists (Ed.).

tenor-player in the band seemed to think that all the tenor parts on my stand were really his whenever a solo was intended.

Finally I went to Geraldo's office to complain. Gerry seemed to be sympathetic and told me that all new arrangements would have the performer's name written on the top of the music parts. That satisfied me until I found that my name didn't appear on any part that had a solo. The last straw, which made me decide to give notice, was at a Sunday evening concert in a cinema theatre. Geraldo never rehearsed the band. He only employed top class players who were expected to be able to read anything at first sight. On my stand for the concert was an arrangement of 'Bugle Call Rag'. As usual, I looked to see what I had to play and, to my amazement, I saw that I had been left the tenor solo, which had been written out in full. I had never seen it before but, being a good reader, I had no qualms until Gerry beat in the tempo. It was breakneck speed and I knew I had my work cut out. In fact I played it faultlessly note for note though I lost a pint of sweat in the process. After the performance the bass player Phil Goody congratulated me. Then the other musicians came up, one by one to do the same.

After that I decided that it was time for me to go. I felt sure that the music had been put on my stand with the thought that I might make a mess of it.

Ambrose and the Palace

Some time later I worked occasionally, on a freelance basis, with another famous orchestra: Ambrose's. Of all the broadcasting bands I heard on the radio in the early thirties before the advent of Lew Stone, Ambrose's was my favourite. I used to listen to their Saturday night broadcasts from the Mayfair Hotel. The band was performing for an elite, socialite clientele but they didn't just play light music. The rhythm came over the air with a feel reminiscent of American bands. [2] The musicians were obviously jazz-orientated and the arrangements were outstanding (I think some of them were done by a publisher-arranger named Stan Bowsher). There were also two excellent singers, Sam Browne (who stayed for a long period) and Elsie Carlisle. The nights Ambrose broadcast were always ones to look forward to. I remember once in Archer Street being told to hurry to buy a record entitled 'My Man of War' sung by Elsie Carlisle. It was going to be withdrawn from stocks because of the *double-entendre* of the lyrics. Like everyone else, I bought a copy. By today's standards it was pretty innocuous.

When the opportunity arose to work with Ambrose I felt proud to be involved with him. From the experience I discovered two things about the maestro. One was that he had a lovely, laid-back sense of humour. The other: there was something indefinable in his personality which seemed to bring out the best from his musicians.

This indefinable quality was apparent at a recording session for which Ambrose asked me to write some arrangements. Of course, at all recording sessions with a big orchestra, it is the arranger who first conducts the band. He knows every note he

---

[2] Bert Ambrose, born in London in 1897, studied violin and worked initially in the United States. In 1927 he was offered the position of musical director at the Mayfair Hotel, London, at the then astonishing salary of £10,000 a year. The band, with its Anglo-American personnel, was an immediate success, broadcasting regularly and recording for Brunswick, HMV and Decca. Ambrose's records and his broadcasts from the Mayfair soon made him a national figure. Albert McCarthy (in *The Dance Band Era*) notes that "as a new decade arrived his reputation as the leader of a dance band with uniquely high standards of musicianship and sophistication spread to Europe and ultimately the United States." Often employing excellent jazz players, his band remained successful for nearly three decades. After a final British tour in 1956, Ambrose worked mainly in show business management (Ed.).

has written, and all the feeling that has been put into such terms as *piano* and *mezzo forte* and often has not been noticed by the instrumentalists the first time round. So I conducted the band as it played through my arrangements. Ambrose sat in the recording booth in the studio, listening carefully and without comment. Then, when the pieces had been run through, over the studio loudspeaker came the words, "OK Harry, you come in here and I'll take over now."

Then a remarkable change took place. Ammy beat in the tempo slightly slower than mine had been. Although the band was playing the same notes, the whole quality had changed. It wasn't just that the tempo was slower. There was a different feeling, almost spiritual in content. The music was changed. I'm sure that it was something in Ammy's personality that the musicians felt and that entered their own.

About Ambrose's sense of humour. I can best illustrate it from something that happened on another occasion. It concerned another tenor sax player named Mossy Kaye who once played beside me for a short time in another band. He had joined Ambrose after having been demobbed from the Armed Forces following a nervous breakdown.

Ambrose's band was playing its first set one evening. During the set Mossy abruptly left the platform. As usual with the big prestigious bands, the bandleader would come on-stage only after the band had played the first set without him. When Ambrose arrived as the band was finishing the first set he looked around and asked, "Where's Mossy?" Someone told him, "Mossy went off without saying anything. He went through the doors to the corridor where the skips are kept." Ammy immediately went out to the linen skips where the dirty linen was collected for washing and found Mossy sitting on one of them with his head in his hands. "What's the matter, Mossy," he asked. Mossy replied, "I can't stand it. I just can't stand it." Ambrose got up, opened the door and stood listening to the band for a while. Then he came back out to the skips and said, "Move over Mossy, neither can I."

The last gig I played for Bert Ambrose was in Buckingham Palace. It was a ball for King George VI and Queen Elizabeth (now the Queen Mother). By that time, as I'll explain later, I had a business operating from Shaftesbury Avenue. I had just left the office there to go for lunch when I met Nat Temple.[3] He asked me if I would like to play for Ambrose at the Palace. I told him I would if I was free. He gave me the date and the time of starting. I said I would be free only up to midnight. The reason was that I had to finish writing an arrangement that had to be with the BBC first thing next morning. Nat assured me that the booking would end around midnight and so I accepted.

On arriving at the Palace, I was conducted to a large room where some of my colleagues had already arrived. Ambrose arrived later and asked us to go to the bandstand. I knew all the chaps. They had been booked specially for this occasion and they were the same musicians, booked from the pool of top players, as had previously played for me in a pick-up band booked by the People's Entertainment Society. This was a section of the Co-operative Movement managed by Bill Sensier. At the time, Bill was also managing the Airshows booking agency which I had been involved in starting.

We started to play and, during our first set, there was a lot of *sotto voce* banter in the band as we compared the conditions in which we were now playing with those in which we had worked for the People's Entertainment Society. Ambrose told us to stop the talking. He was angry with all the irreverent comments. "It's dustbins with lids off," he said to us, meaning that our talk stank. He had worked all his life with what he

---

[3] Saxophonist Nat Temple was working in bands in the Armed Forces during the war, but also played engagements with the bands of both Geraldo and Ambrose before his demobilisation in 1946 (Ed.)

thought of as the upper crust of society and we were lowering the tone with our working class chatter. At first I thought he was joking and laughed. But he wasn't and I was reprimanded.

We played for an hour and then had a break during which another band played and we were served food and wine. We returned for our second session only to discover that Ambrose had left for his regular job and Sid Simone was there to lead the band for the rest of the night. Sid was a violinist, a better performer than Ambrose, and we played for another hour before returning to the room for another break which ended at midnight. I began to get worried. I asked Sid what time we would finish but he said, "I don't know." We played for another hour, which took us to one o'clock. Then I knew that the ball would continue until some time in the morning so I told Sid I would have to leave and explained why. I said that I had only been booked until midnight and that I had to finish writing an arrangement. I picked up my instruments, went to the room where the instrument cases were left, packed and went home. From then on, my name was mud. I had walked out on the King and Queen! That was unheard of. I was also told that I wasn't going to get paid.

I phoned Ambrose's office the next day and told the secretary that I wanted to talk to him. I said that I needed to explain what had happened. He agreed to see me in his flat in Mayfair at 3.00 p.m. On arrival, I was surprised to see him wearing his pyjamas and a dressing gown. He said, "I'm having breakfast. Would you like some kippers?" I said, "No thanks, but I'd like some coffee." When that arrived he asked, "What's the problem?" I explained what had happened and that I had been told I was not going to be paid. I said that, if that was so, I would have to report the matter to the Musicians' Union. He smiled and said, "Go to the office. The money is waiting for you." I thanked him, shook hands and left. When I arrived at the office I was given the same amount as the rest of the musicians who had worked until 5.00 a.m.!

Leaving aside the Geraldo period, work as a regular, full-time instrumentalist with the big orchestras mainly gave way to other things after I ended the period of touring with Oscar Rabin at the end of 1942. With Oscar, I had been able to set up the Pieces of Eight as a band within the band and I wanted to find a way to keep that small group idea alive and to develop it. From around 1943, I gradually edged towards a situation where I could operate successfully as a freelance and eventually run a band playing music in the style I wanted, and a music business of my own. But it was a slow process.

Doubloon

On the arranging front, I initially contacted Wally Wallond (the head of the BBC's arranging department) to tell him that I was available for anything he had to offer. He immediately began to give me orders for arrangements for the BBC (a few years later it was Wally's desk that I had to get my arrangement to when I 'walked out' on Ambrose and the King and Queen at the Palace). He also offered me some gigs he had as pianist-leader. In his band was a wonderful double bass player and arranger named Peter Akister. Although they were society gigs, we were also able to play some jazz and the work was both enjoyable and profitable.

One winter's night, travelling in Wally's car back home after a late gig, the roads were saturated with heavy rain and partially thawed snow. We were stopped by a motorist travelling towards us who told us that the road further on was impassable. We decided to chance it and, sure enough, we arrived at a hollow that was flooded by an overflow from the river. Wally, being the tallest, got out, rolled up his dress trousers and walked into the water to estimate the depth. He thought we might make it, got back in and drove on. But the car stopped in the middle of the deepest part. The water had reached the bottom of the doors and covered the exhaust. Hence the stop. There was nothing we could do except follow Wally's example, roll our trousers up to our thighs, get into the water and push.

My middle name being shorty, the water came up much higher on me, which didn't do my dress trousers a lot of good. Also the water was freezing, which came as a shock to my system. Anyway, we got the car out, got back in with very cold, wet feet and prayed that the car would start. It did! With a sigh of relief we drove home none the worse for wear.

During this time I was trying to build the Pieces of Eight, which was initially just the idea of a small band of my own established during the time with Oscar, into a working unit. I managed to get the occasional gig and recruited musicians from the Archer Street pool when required. Because I had preserved my original arrangements, the style stayed the same irrespective of who was in the band at any given time.

When I got an offer, through a well-known agent, to play a week in a hotel in Whitehaven I thought I was on my way up as a bandleader. The engagement entailed playing nightly in the ballroom of the Empress Hotel. We travelled to Whitehaven by train. In those days train travel was not expensive and had the advantage that professional bands, concert parties and theatrical shows could reserve complete compartments. As there were ten of us (including two wives) I was able to reserve two compartments.

On the way, Johnny Wise, who besides being the drummer was one of my close friends, asked if I had a signature tune. I hadn't thought it would be necessary, but Johnny pointed out that every band at that time had one. I decided to write one. Most bands used an already published tune (as Roy Fox had used 'Whispering') but I felt it would be better if mine were original. While I sat in one of the compartments listening to the noise of the wheels making a kind of rhythm, my mind began to wander almost to the point of being lulled to sleep. I came to, with a start, and thoughts of "What would be appropriate? What kind of tune should it be?" And suddenly the germ of an idea began to develop. The band's name Pieces of Eight conjured up thoughts of pirates, the Spanish Main, buccaneers and doubloons, 'Yo ho ho and a bottle of rum' and there was a ready made tune waiting to be put on to paper. 'Doubloon' was being born. By the time we reached Whitehaven the theme and band parts were ready to be performed. The hotel's advertisement ran:

> EMPRESS BALLROOM, WHITEHAVEN. Enormous Success. England's leading tenor saxophonist HARRY GOLD and His Pieces of Eight. Hear the band playing their new signature tune 'Doubloon' composed in Whitehaven by Harry Gold. Special half-hour JAM SESSION at each dance. Featuring each player, a master of his instrument.

The personnel was George McCullum (piano), Harry Benson (double bass), Johnny Wise (drums), 'Flash' Shields (trumpet), Rick Kennedy (trombone), Harry Gerrard (alto sax and clarinet), and myself on tenor and bass saxes. My youngest sister Sylvia was brought in to sing a few popular songs of the day.

After a successful and enjoyable week, it was back to London in search of the occasional gig and writing more arrangements for the BBC arranging department. But a phone call from Wally Wallond led to a change of direction. Wally asked me to write a score that was needed for delivery the following morning by 9.00 a.m. He said, "I'm afraid it's a big one and you'll need help. There's a chap named Norrie Paramor who works as a freelance for the department. Give him a ring." So I called Norrie and we worked together through the night. The completed job led to a long and fruitful friendship. We discovered that we had a similar style of writing and both of us were versed in orchestral scoring as well as jazz and dance band styles.[4]

The first stage in the development of our association was an agreement to pool our connections. Almost immediately, we began to get more work. That made it essential to have an office and a music copyist. We found accommodation in a building in Shaftesbury Avenue which was sufficient for our needs at the time, and engaged as copyist Benny Keen, a tenor sax player who worked in Oscar Rabin's band. He and his wife had shared lodgings with Peggy and me in Weston while we were both with Oscar and he had worked as a copyist for me when I was writing arrangements for the Rabin band.

Things were going well. Suddenly I got the chance to do some broadcasts. I'd been trying to get broadcasts for some time but it had been like coming up against a brick wall with no door. First of all I had made contact with Tawny Neilson, head of BBC dance band programmes. She asked me, "Are you making any records?" When I said I was not, she replied, "When you are recording, come and see me." At the same time, Norrie and I had been doing a lot of arrangements for the

---

[4] Norrie Paramor, born in London in 1913, had played piano with various dance bands during the 1930s. During and after World War II he was with Harry Gold's Pieces of Eight as featured pianist for some five years (broken by war service in which he was an arranger for the Air Force Entertainment Unit). In 1952 he became recording director for EMI's Columbia record label. In the late 1950s and early 1960s he was Britain's most successful producer of popular music records, responsible for many hit recordings by singers such as Cliff Richard, Frank Ifield, Helen Shapiro and Billy Fury. He also arranged and produced numerous 'easy-listening' orchestral albums issued under his own name, and from 1972 to 1978 was director of the BBC Midland Radio Orchestra. According to the *Guinness Who's Who*, "Paramor remains one of the most underrated figures in the history of UK pop [music] and a posthumous reappraisal of his work is overdue." (Ed.).

Peter Maurice Music Company in Denmark Street. The company contact for HMV Records, Wally Ridley, was equally helpful when I approached him about recording. "Are you doing any broadcasting?" he asked. "Try and get on the air and then I'll see what I can do." A real 'Catch 22' situation.

Calypso Style

The much needed break which got me in to broadcasting came from Pat Dixon, a BBC producer, for whom I had written many arrangements. He introduced me to another producer, Elizabeth Tyson, who was starting an overseas programme to be broadcast to the West Indies. She needed a bandleader who could also arrange the music required for the programme. It was to be a weekly broadcast with singers and West Indian Forces personnel, who would broadcast messages to their homes.

Some of the tunes to be used would be calypso style, so I found it necessary to use West Indian musicians. I engaged saxophonist Freddy Grant, pianist York Da Sousa and guitarist Lauderic Caton. They all knew West Indian melodies and the intricate rhythms necessary for authentic performance of the music.[5] The group was augmented with trumpet, double bass and drums to accompany singers who would be engaged for the show by the producer. Jack Coles, who later became

---

[5] Grant, Da Sousa and Caton had settled in Britain in 1937, 1935 and 1940 respectively. Grant is best remembered now for his collaboration with trumpeter Humphrey Lyttleton in the Grant-Lyttleton Paseo Band of the early 1950s. In the mid-1940s he was working with drummer Carlo Krahmer's bands and Leslie 'Jiver' Hutchinson. Pianist-arranger Da Souza worked extensively with Hutchinson's band in the 1940s and later. Caton was leading a trio at the Caribbean Club in London during the mid-1940s (Ed.).

conductor of the BBC Midland Orchestra, was the trumpet player and my cousin Harry Benson was on bass. Drummers were brought in from the Archer Street pool as required.

Apart from the music, the programme had news of what was going on in the various West Indian islands. This was read by Ernest Eytle, a barrister, and the brother of Tommy Eytle of the 'East Enders' television soap opera.

Completing the permanent entertainment personnel were three singers, Ida Shepley, Edric Connor and Rita Williams. They preferred to plan their songs for the following week immediately after transmission. I was all in favour of that. It meant that keys and routines could be agreed while we were in the studio. That was an excellent time saver, particularly in view of the fact that I would have to attend a conference a couple of days before each show. This was to meet and consult with additional artistes who happened to be in town and were booked for the show.

All of the orchestrations were paid for by the BBC, which was a lucrative situation, though often it meant sitting up all night working on the arrangements. But the job was both enjoyable and educative, though sometimes it was a little difficult because of differences of opinion between Liz Tyson and her West Indian counterpart Una Marson. That sometimes led to my opinion being sought. Liz wanted more popular songs of the period and some jazz, while Una wanted more calypsos. I needed the patience of a saint and the wisdom of Solomon!

Eventually, when requests from listeners started to come in, Liz was proved right. So the style of presentation changed as well as the personnel. I brought in Norrie Paramor on piano and asked Jack Coles, our trumpeter, if he could recommend a trombonist who could play jazz as well as being a good reader. Jack was in the band of the King's Royal Rifles. He suggested Geoff Love who was in the same band. So Geoff came in and became part of the organisation, although he was still in the services. He was no stranger to me as I had met him previously when he was playing in Freddie Platt's band in a dance hall near Geoff's home town, Todmorden in Yorkshire, around 1935.[6]

This was the moment I had been waiting for. I saw at once that I could build a dixieland-style band by introducing a clarinet to the instrumentation I already had. When I mentioned the idea to Liz Tyson she was enthusiastic. She discussed the proposal with Una Marson and, to my surprise, Una went for it wholeheartedly. So Freddy Grant switched from his alto sax to clarinet to play the dixieland numbers. We went under the unlikely name of the 'Pocomaniacs' for the purposes of the West Indies broadcasts.

Pat Dixon, the producer who had introduced me to Liz and the West Indies programme, had started a weekly programme on the BBC Home Service which he called 'Jazz Is Where You Find It'. The title reflected his thinking that there were many different styles of jazz in existence and that the variety of styles and personal taste among them is all part of the enjoyment of jazz. I was in complete accord with that line of thought and we had several meetings to discuss possibilities for me to do arrangements for the programme. He contacted some leading instrumentalists who would lead bands playing in styles of their choice. Nat Temple, Ted Heath, Chic Smith and Kenny Baker were some of the names involved.

I was not given the opportunity to lead a band on the programme because, thanks to Pat, I already had the West

---

[6] Geoff Love, born in 1918, was the son of an American dancer who settled in Britain. He played with Freddie Platt at the Carlton Ballroom, Rochdale in 1935, before moving to London. He was with the King's Royal Rifles from 1941 to 1946. After demobilisation he was with Harry Gold's Pieces of Eight from the summer of 1946 until 1949. In later years he led his own orchestra on television and radio and for recordings (Ed.)

Indies show, even though it was not broadcast on the Home Service. But he asked me to write many of the arrangements that were used on 'Jazz Is Where You Find It', and that kept me in contact with the BBC booking department.

While the war was still continuing musicians were called up to serve in the armed forces so it was very difficult to maintain a permanent personnel. That meant that unless the arrangements were carefully written, the band's style could change according to the style of the players booked. Hence the need to write everything the way I wanted it played. It worked.

Paramor-Gold

With Norrie Paramor and me working together on arranging assignments, the Paramor Gold Orchestral Service was born. We advertised in the *Melody Maker* for music copyists with some knowledge of orchestration. After testing several applicants we chose two, Bernard Ebbinghouse and Ron Goodwin, who had been working as copyists for Campbell and Connelly, the music publishers. Ron was also a trumpet player so, occasionally, he played with the Pieces of Eight.[7]

Fate was spinning its web with ever-widening strands. Norrie received his call-up papers and joined the Air Force Entertainment Unit which had, among its personnel, actors, singers and comedians, and a theatrical agent named Cecil Buckingham. He and Norrie got together to produce shows for

[7] Goodwin, born in 1925, worked as a copyist and staff arranger for music publishers and as arranger for Stanley Black, Geraldo and Ted Heath, before forming his own broadcasting concert orchestra in 1951. In the 1950s he had a series of orchestral hit records and began writing film scores, providing the music during the 1960s and 1970s for over sixty films, including *Those Magnificent Men in Their Flying Machines* (1965), *Where Eagles Dare* (1968) and Hitchcock's *Frenzy* (1972) (Ed.).

the Entertainment Unit, using well known variety acts who were already in Air Force blue. Cecil was a partner in an theatrical agency called Buckingham and Wingrove. The upshot of Norrie's contact with him was that we rented to Buckingham and Wingrove two of our rooms in Shaftesbury Avenue and also agreed an unofficial partnership arrangement with them whereby we would write all the arrangements for their clients and, if required, scripts for sketches. The theatrical agency, in turn, provided band work, so all in all it was a profitable arrangement which served us in good stead after the war when Norrie and Cecil returned to civvy street. One of the people we did work for under this agreement was Ralph Reader who became well known for his 'gang shows' and later for the Boy Scout shows. We were responsible for arranging two of his signature tunes.

During the final period of the war, the Pieces of Eight continued to broadcast weekly for the BBC West Indies programme. The band also got work broadcasting overseas, more generally, from Bush House in the Strand for the BBC's world-wide service. One of the final recruits to the Pieces became integrated as a permanent member by accident. It happened through Harry Francis, who was then the Musicians Union organiser. He had to attend a band contest at Chatham and asked if I would go along as a judge. One of the competing groups was a naval jazz band featuring a cornettist, Cyril Ellis, who came from Glasgow. He was brilliant. After the proceedings had ended I talked with him and discovered that he had considerable periods of leave from his naval duties. When I asked if he would play for the Pieces of Eight, he stood for a while open-mouthed in disbelief. But I knew he was the right man for the job. During the war period we had to use anyone who was available and that included Cyril, thanks to his leave periods. He eventually became a regular member after his demobilisation.[8]

Around this time, the band had a great breakthrough as far as popular recognition was concerned. It happened through an appearance at one of the Jazz Jamborees organised by the Musicians' Social and Benevolent Council. The Jamborees had been running annually with great success, all of the bands giving their services without fee to help swell the benevolent fund. But there wasn't much jazz because most of the volunteers were dance bands. One year, however, a band that had agreed to play dropped out of the programme at the last minute. There was the problem of finding a replacement at very short notice.

An emergency meeting was called to resolve the problem. During the discussion one of the members said, "Harry, you've got a band, haven't you?" I replied that I had. "Could you do it?" he asked. I said we were available, and we were in. My brother Laurie was in the army in the Pioneer Corps, but he had been seconded to an entertainment unit in London under the leadership of Eric Robinson. So he was roped in for the programme.

We had to play three numbers on a platform that would rise from below stage while a big band was setting up. After deciding what tunes we would play, I suggested that we should rehearse the pieces until we knew the arrangements well enough to play from memory. I pointed out that there might be

[8] Cyril Ellis, born in 1923, served in the Royal Navy from 1944 to 1946 and worked in Claude Giddins' band while stationed at Chatham in 1946. He worked regularly with the Pieces of Eight from his demobilisation (May 1946) until January 1949. He was with Sid Phillips' orchestra from 1949 until 1954, playing also with Carlo Krahmer at the 1949 Paris Jazz Festival, and with the Jazz Today Unit in 1953. After leaving full time playing he worked for Boosey and Hawkes, the musicial instrument makers, but gigged occasionally with Harry Gold and others in the 1960s (Ed.).

problems setting up on a narrow platform with little room for music stands.

I shall never forget the wonderful reaction by the audience. The show was at the Dominion Theatre, Tottenham Court Road. Most of what had gone before was swingy popular tunes of the day, and as the 'lift' moved upwards to the sound of rehearsed traditional jazz in dixieland style, we heard a roar of applause from a full theatre, which was deafening. At the end of our third number the platform started to move downwards to the sound of cheers and hand clapping never to be forgotten. The newspaper reports of the band's performance were glowing and, soon afterwards, we were inundated with calls from booking agents offering work.

The tide had changed but the rapid development of the two sides of the business (arranging/orchestration, on the one hand, and performing with the band, on the other) was taking its toll on Norrie on me. Apart from everything else, we had regular radio shows to write for. These included Lou Praeger's Saturday night dance broadcast at the Hammersmith Palais. Each week, for this, there would always be one new tune submitted by songwriters from all over the country in a kind of song contest. Generally the writers were amateurs. Though they were able to write the melody out on paper, they could not orchestrate it and that was where we came in. One of the songs submitted was a waltz composed by two women who were completely unknown as songwriters. It became a number one popular hit record. The title was 'Cruising Down the River'. As far I know they never wrote another song.

We tried to offload a bit of the pressure of our business by delegating. Ron Goodwin was developing his arranging talents to the point where Norrie and I felt confident that we could allow him to orchestrate one of the tunes for Lou Praeger. Our work load was almost at breaking point so we explained to Ron the routine required but allowed him complete freedom in carrying out the job.

The upshot was that Praeger phoned the following Monday in a not very friendly mood saying that he expected Norrie or me to do his arrangements, and if we couldn't do them he would find someone else who could. I couldn't understand how he knew that we hadn't written the arrangement for him. Norrie and I had both vetted Ron's score and were sure that it was really well done. I came to the conclusion that somehow Ron must have let the word out that he had written the arrangement.

The bombing had begun again, with V1 flying bombs and V2 rockets landing on London. Norrie and I decided that it would be best if our families left the city. It was no place for the children. Norrie's wife Joan went to her parents in Liverpool and Peggy to hers in Bradford, leaving Norrie and me to fend for ourselves. As Norrie's home was in Norbury (south London) and mine was central in Holborn, we thought it would be convenient to use mine as much as possible.

With our families away, we took on some additional work in the orchestral pit at the Piccadilly Theatre, in an American musical show called 'Panama Hattie'. It was an excellent show with a fine cast, including the American comedienne-singer Bebe Daniels, Claude Hulbert (brother of musical revue star Jack Hulbert), Max Wall and Richard Hearne (who later became famous as 'Mr. Pastry' on BBC television). The theatre was in Denman Street, a side street at the junction of Regent Street and Piccadilly Circus, adjacent to the Regent Palace Hotel. The working times fitted in well with our office hours apart from the Wednesday matinée, when we could leave the office safely in the hands of our staff for a couple of hours. The extra work helped to ease the evening loneliness while our families were away.

The flying bomb blitz went on as usual but by now we were used to that. One night a bomb exploded on the roof of the Regent Palace Hotel and damaged part of the stage and the orchestra area in the Piccadilly Theatre. On arrival for the first show next evening, we discovered that the theatre was closed and the orchestra pit was covered by a mound of rubble. We were told that the show wouldn't be continuing after that.[9] I had always taken my instruments home at night so, of course, they were safe. But I had left in the theatre the special stand which held them during the performance. It must have been somewhere under the rubble and I never recovered it. *C'est la vie.*

The war situation had changed dramatically, of course, by the spring of 1945. The Normandy landings had been successful and the Allied advance had freed Paris. Norrie's unit had been ordered to do a short spell abroad and I held the fort in the office, with the assistance of our staff. One day, en route for the Coach and Horses pub during my lunch break, I met Eric Winstone, full of worry. He told me that he was just about to set off with his band to the Continent to entertain the troops for ENSA and one of his tenor sax players had let him down.[10] ENSA (Entertainment National Service Association) was a Government-sponsored organisation to provide entertainment for men and women serving in the armed forces abroad. I told Eric I would go with him, providing Norrie agreed to this. I suggested to Norrie that, because there was little work, we should close the office for the six weeks I would be away and

---

[9] In fact the theatre stayed closed effectively for the rest of the war. It reopened in 1945 with Agatha Christie's play 'Appointment with Death' (Ed.)

[10] Born in London in 1913, Winstone had, in 1941, formed a big band which achieved wide broadcasting and recording success. After serving briefly in the RAF he led his own band on many ENSA tours during the war. For two decades from 1946 he played summer seasons at holiday camps and was a musical director at Southern Television (Ed.)

put the staff on half pay. He agreed and off I went to the 'second front'.

Brussels-Paris 1945

I had to get myself kitted out in uniform. All personnel employed by ENSA had to wear military uniform. Partly this was because it was thought there would be resentment among the troops if the entertainers were dressed in civilian clothes. Another more valid reason was that if we had been captured by the enemy and were not wearing uniform we might have been considered to be spies and that could have been very serious. So we were given army uniforms and the rank of lieutenant (incidentally, I don't know why we say 'leftenant'; there's no EFFIN lieutenant!). We also had cards saying that, if captured, we were to be treated as officers, according to the Geneva Convention. There was a minor problem for me because of my bad feet. I couldn't wear the standard military footwear. "No problem," said ENSA. I was given the address of a Greek orthopaedic shoe maker who would make two pairs of shoes for me, to be paid for by the authorities.

Fully kitted out, I met the rest of the band at Tilbury and we boarded the boat which turned out to be a troopship bound for Ostend. All the way across the Channel we were guarded by a couple of small naval boats which made us realise that we weren't going on a holiday. While we were en route Eric suggested that we should play a concert for the troops on board. It would relieve the boredom and possibly the nervous tension too. So we readily agreed. The reaction from the soldiers was phenomenal and before we landed at Ostend we were all invited to the mess for drinks.

Arriving in Ostend harbour we saw the results of the Allied bombing. It was devastating. As far as I could see, there wasn't a building standing in the harbour area. We disembarked and were taken to Brussels, to a hotel where we were to be quartered for the next three days.

During that period, the drummer, Johnny Marks, disappeared. We were all very worried about him because we were soon to be moved to another destination and he would have no idea where we had gone. We ourselves didn't know the destination, given the need for secrecy. There was also the possibility that he might have been injured or captured. But Johnny must have had his own secret service organisation. He turned up three days later at the hotel where we had been billeted. He said he had met some friends of his and decided to stay with them. I think he had been doing a bit of black marketeering.[11]

Apart from Johnny, Eric's band was eighteen strong. That included the four singers: Alan Kane and his sister Gloria, Julie Dawn and a very young and pretty blonde woman named Hazel Bray, on whom Eric Winstone had a crush. I don't remember the names of most of the band musicians, apart from the saxophone section, who were close friends. There was Harry Conn, George Glover (also a photographer), John Arslanian, and myself on tenor.

During that billeting period in Brussels, Eric tried to entice Hazel. The information that he was planning this came from Hazel herself. So some of us in the band planned to lumber Eric when Hazel told us that she had been asked to go to his bedroom. We found places to hide in the bedroom, including a large cupboard, the wardrobe and even under the bed. When Hazel arrived, we waited until Eric got to work. Then, when a nervous, high pitched scream from Hazel was heard, we knew

---

[11] Johnny Marks had worked for several years with Lou Praeger's band and recorded in London with Fats Waller in 1939. During the war years he worked with Nat Gonella, Maurice Winnick and others. He died, aged 47, in 1955 (Ed.).

it was time to act. We all emerged laughing our heads off and were confronted by an utterly dumbfounded Eric. It was a lumber to end all lumbers.

At the hotel in Brussels I met Peter Packay, a well known Belgian bandleader, composer and arranger.[12] We had a long discussion about how conditions had been during the German Occupation. The beer was good too! Peter told me that if we ever got to Paris we should make sure we visited the Sphinx club. As he explained, "It's a night club and the waitresses wear nothing except a bit of dangling cloth in front of their lower regions." But I dismissed that idea because none of us knew where we were going or whether we would ever reach Paris.

Eric Winstone was a friendly guy, who unfortunately suffered from a mild form of chorea (St. Vitus' Dance). If he was engaged in conversation, seated at a table, he would suddenly put his fingers down and beat a tapping movement all the way across the surface and eventually down the table leg. It caused much amused amazement. Sometimes he would beat his shoulder with some force as though he was punishing himself for some remembered sin. He also had a bad stammer, but all of those quirks or problems would disappear as soon as he was on stage in front of an audience.

At rehearsal he would use a pencil as an improvised baton. But it was never his own pencil. All of us in the band carried pencils to mark parts of arrangements that needed altering. Inevitably, Eric would ask for a pencil and inevitably the

---

[12] Peter Packay (Pierre Pacquet), born in Brussels in 1904, had taken up trumpet in 1924 despite an accident that left him without the use of one of his arms. He became an arranger and composer and leader of the group Bistrouille ADO in 1927. Later he formed Packay's Swing Academy, which accompanied Coleman Hawkins in Brussels. After the war he abandoned trumpet playing and worked solely as a composer and arranger (Ed.)

pencil would go flying off in any direction, never to be returned, as he conducted.

We were never really in any danger from the fighting because we were always several miles behind the front lines. Only once was there the possibility of being hurt. It was while we were playing at an Air Force camp. There was some shelling and we were told to keep down for a while. Apparently, because of the speed of the Allied advance, a pocket of Germans had been cornered near the coast. Every hour or so they would fire a few shells in defiance.

We entertained tired troops at Nijmegen, Arnhem and other towns and we crossed the Rhine over a Bailey bridge. We also volunteered to play at hospitals, apart from our schedule of regular performances. The word was passed on that we were to be given an extra week in Paris as recompense. While there, we were able to travel around to see the sights using the Metro free of charge. It seemed that everyone in uniform was given that privilege.

Then I remembered the Sphinx! A small group of us decided to visit it. We found out which line to use and the station from which to alight. When we left the train, however, we were faced with a maze of passages with no information about the Sphinx. I saw a middle-aged lady walking ahead and chanced my arm. I ran up to her and demanded, "Où est la Sphinx?" She stopped, wagged her finger and said in English, "Naughty, naughty! I will show you." And that was that.

Outside the entrance were two American military policemen standing guard, but they ignored us so we went inside and asked if we could get in to the club. "No," was the response. "It is forbidden, but ask the police outside." We did but the police told us that it was nothing to do with them. They were on duty there just to prevent American soldiers entering. So we tried once more by asking for the manager, who turned out to be a manageress. After explaining to her that we were not

Americans but British musicians we were allowed in. There was a lavishly decorated restaurant with a long bar at the entrance and several rows of tables and chairs in the main room. In that area there were some young ladies lounging around. Yes, you've guessed it. They were completely nude except for a narrow loin cloth and our eyes were coming out like organ stops. We stood at the bar and ordered a round of cognac which tasted like methylated spirits and cost an 'arm and a leg'. One of the young ladies came over to us and became very friendly, making with the body language. We then decided that the whole set up was clearly a brothel. We had just ordered another round of cognac when the manageress ran to us in a panic, saying, "Quick, hide! The colonel is here. You will get me into trouble." Dutifully, we hid in a recess near the bar until we got the 'all clear' and decided to leave.

So there we were, in May 1945, in Paris. We were asked if we would play for some wounded soldiers in a nearby hospital, which of course we did. While we were in one of the wards, the BBC's Tawny Neilson came in, having been sent over to Paris to arrange some broadcast messages. She told us, "The war's over. The Germans have surrendered. How would you like to broadcast to England from the grounds of the British Embassy, Paris, on the very day the war ended?" It seemed a very good idea, especially with all the festive noise going on in the background. For us in the band it was an exciting and historic occasion.

As we were not soldiers, we began to think about making arrangements to go home. While we were waiting for information and the possibility of transport, I made some inquiries about whether or not the famous Selmer firm, makers of saxes and clarinets, was still operating. They were based in Paris, and I discovered that they had kept going right through the war. I had no doubt that they would have been left alone by the German occupying forces because the occupiers too needed instruments. John Arslanian knew Paris very well because his parents had lived there for most of their lives. So he took me to the Selmer shop and I bought a pair of clarinets at bargain prices. We had been given a regular allowance of gin, whisky and 200 cigarettes a month. So I traded the cigarettes and gin for cash and used it buy the clarinets. Then, when we were told that we would be returning to Britain in a few days, I packed my case, including the Selmers, and waited with bated breath for the day and time of departure. I wanted to get back home.

The flight was on an American paratroop plane which landed at Croydon. We sat side by side on a long wooden trestle-type seat. But there were no complaints about discomfort, just delight that we were going home. After landing we had to go through customs to make the usual declaration. The only person who didn't get through was Johnny Marks, who had been dealing in various black market operations. His bass drum was packed with goods that were difficult to obtain in England, and he was forced to open up. The whole lot was confiscated.

So it was back to the office in Shaftesbury Avenue and work again. While I had been away my West Indies programme had continued, with BBC permission, under the directorship of Jack Coles. Eventually, Norrie, Jack and Geoff Love were 'demobbed' (demobilised from the armed services). The number of dance gigs was beginning to increase. Also we were kept busy writing arrangements for the stage acts of artistes who were also being demobbed and who were signed to Buckingham and Wingrove's theatrical agency.

6.

PIECES OF EIGHT: ON THE AIR AND ON THE ROAD

Luck, or fate's finger spinning its web, intruded again. I was walking along New Bond Street towards the Aeolian Hall, which was where the light music and arranging department of the BBC was situated. I had an orchestration to deliver there. Coming towards me I saw the normally unapproachable Tawny Neilson, the head of the BBC's Dance Band Department. She called out, "Hello Harry! Come and have a drink." I was so amazed by the invitation that for a few minutes I forgot the orchestration I was carrying and walked with her to a nearby pub. Then I realised that I had better deliver my music, which was needed urgently, so I told Tawny I'd be back in a few minutes. I ran to the Aeolian, made the delivery and ran back to the pub *alactrissimo*. By that time she was drinking a Scotch (a beverage of which she was very fond indeed). She bought me one and said, "I've got a date for you. Come up to the office and we'll talk about it."

I couldn't believe what I was hearing. It had seemed impossible before to get my own broadcasts without having records. But now there was no insistence on records, just a straightforward offer of broadcasts on the BBC Home Service. Perhaps she felt grateful to me because I had helped her by persuading the musicians in Eric Winstone's band to do the broadcast on VE Day, which must have been a feather in her cap. Whatever the reason, from then on, the Pieces of Eight were able to broadcast regularly, although we couldn't do jazz. We did broadcasts with dance music and popular ballad-type songs of the day, though sometimes in dixieland-style arrangements.

Suddenly the impasse had ended. In December 1945 Wally Ridley came up trumps with a recording date for the Parlophone recording company. Norrie Paramor and I discussed the situation and decided to use some different musicians from those playing the gigs. The personnel on that first recording was Duncan Whyte (trumpet), Laurie Clarke (trombone), my brother Laurie and myself both on tenor saxes, Ralph Bruce (clarinet), Norrie on piano, Freddy Phillips (guitar), Sid Heiger (drums) and Harry Benson (double bass).[1] We felt that it would be necessary to have musicians who were used to recording studio technique. Young Cyril Ellis, while being a good player, was not yet ready for recording and the brilliant Duncan Whyte had played for many bands and recordings.[2] Laurie Clarke, a fine session musician but not as good a jazz player as Geoff Love, was the trombonist on our early recording sessions because Geoff's army commitments meant he was only available for some of the time. The clarinettist Ralph Bruce was an excellent player with a soft tone and relaxed style. He had become a regular member when we started doing our Home Service broadcasts. Bert Weedon was another early recruit to the regular personnel. He joined the band as guitarist in 1946, staying with the Pieces for about two years.

---

[1] The Pieces of Eight first recorded with this personnel on December 14th 1945. Six titles (*Sentimental Journey*, *Meander In The Minor*, *Lazy River*, *Doubloon*, *Oh You Beautiful Doll* and *Kentucky*) were issued on record from this and two subsequent Parlophone recording sessions in January and February 1946 (Ed.)

[2] Whyte, born in Glasgow in 1910, played with many bands, including Percival Mackey, Lou Praeger, Billy Mason and Teddy Joyce, through the 1930s and 1940s and led his own bands, mainly in Scotland, in the post-war years, freelancing from the 1960s (Ed.).

Politics and Plugging

The BBC broadcast booking which Tawny Neilson had arranged with me turned out to be something of an experiment as far as she was concerned. It was for a programme called 'Music While You Work', originally planned by the Government to improve production during the war. The programme seemed to be successful in its objective, but most of the music played was popular music of the day presented in a continuous dirge. Tawny's experiment was to discover whether or not the dixieland style would be suitable.

Letters of approval from listeners began to pour in. Consequently, I was given a string of broadcasting dates which lasted for three months and thereafter bookings for gigs ensued. As the band became more popular, my brother Laurie decided to leave Eric Robinson and become a regular member of the Pieces.[3] This was forced on him by a BBC edict which prohibited broadcasting bandleaders using musicians who were in other bandleaders' personnel.

This edict was partly to serve the BBC's interests in being able to broadcast bands with distinct identity, rather than groups with interchangeable or shared personnel. But it was probably also a consequence of the bandleaders' pressure on the BBC to protect their interests. While the war was on it had

[3] After his demobilisation from the army, Laurie had been playing tenor sax with Eric Robinson's Blue Rockets and George Clouston before joining the Pieces of Eight. He had started on alto sax at the age of 16 and, in the 1930s, worked with Stan Atkins, Lew Foster and Johnny Claes. During the war he played in in the Pioneer Corps Band, George Melachrino's AEF Band and the Blue Rockets. He was with the Pieces of Eight from early 1946 untll late 1952, then worked in band management, but rejoined Harry's band and took over leadership of it from 1956 to 1959 and for a period in the early 1960s (Ed.).

become necessary to follow the practice of using musicians from what became a pool, because of the general shortage of players. As musicians became demobbed more were available, but bandleaders became more protective of their rights as employers. They had started in that way by forming a Danceband Leaders Association. Naturally, I became a member and a Council member. I thought it important that as a trade unionist I should belong to a protective organisation. I was concerned about the possibility of the Danceband Leaders Association becoming a weapon against playing musicians. Of course, I was a playing musician myself. At first, the Association had been organised to protect members from the BBC but, as it became more powerful, it began to drive down rates of pay for musicians, which was what I had anticipated.

I pointed out to the Council that bandleaders were also musicians and therefore they ought to be members of the Musicians' Union. I made it clear that, although they employed musicians, they in turn were employed by the owners of hotels, restaurants and record companies and so they should support the MU and not be in opposition to it. Lew Stone, who was the Chairman, supported me in that suggestion. Eventually, recognising the wisdom of the proposal, dance bandleaders joined the union as individual members and the title of the leaders' organisation was changed to become the Music Directors' Section of the Musicians' Union.

It was a period when music publishers paid bandleaders to play their songs on radio; a system that became known as 'plugging'. The idea was that if a tune was played frequently on the air, the tune would become popular. Plugging wasn't a new thing. It was done during summer seasons at seaside resorts. The most famous of these was Blackpool, where publishers had kiosks with a piano installed and a singer on hand to sing the tunes that the publisher wanted popularised. Plugging on radio was much more intense. Eventually, the

BBC clamped down and put a limit on the number of times a tune could be played.[4] I'm convinced the practice of plugging still goes on, particularly on television. Of course I have no proof, but I recognise similarities.

In August 1945 I received a letter from someone in the armed forces. The letterhead read 'THE EDWARD KASSNER MUSIC CO. LTD' and gave the address as 'c/o Performing Right Society Ltd'. It was signed by '13117457 Sgt E. Kassner, 53 Med Regt RA, BAOR' (British Army of the Rhine). The letter said that Sgt. Kassner would like me to broadcast a number entitled 'You're Made For Me'. He was prepared to pay for the arrangement and a sum of £6 for plugging the tune. I discussed the matter with Norrie Paramor, who thought we could be on to a good thing.

We did include the number in our next broadcast and, in due course, a cheque arrived attached to the following letter:

Dear Harry,

Thanks a lot for last night's broadcast of YOU'RE MADE FOR ME. Please find enclosed cheque in payment for your arrangement.

I do hope you will soon programme the number again, as this helps me to get as much concentration as possible. How do you like DISTRACTION by Ivon de Bie? I would be very pleased if you could give me an airing on this number?

As soon as you have the score of your own composition, which you promised me ready, I should be very pleased if you could send to me immediately, as I need some new numbers for the Continent. Publication

---

[4] The BBC was seriously concerned about song plugging in the years immediately after the war. In 1947 it reached an agreement with the Music Publishers' Association (to be implemented from April 1948) that all plugging would stop in return for an undertaking from the BBC to impose a 60% quota of current songs in its dance music programmes. There was also pressure from the Songwriters' Guild (founded in 1947) that 'current songs' should be, as far as possible, British, to stem what it saw as the American 'cultural invasion' (Ed.)

on the Continent is of considerable value to you, as English music is in demand and they pay good General Fees.

Many thanks again and all the very Best to you and Norrie.

I remain Yours very Sincerely, Eddie R. pp. Edward Kassner Music Co Ltd. 61 Edith Road W14.

As the letter suggests, another source of financial assistance was provided by publishers offering to publish bandleaders' compositions. In this case, publishing our numbers was all part of the inducement for plugging the publisher's compositions while being paid for writing arrangements of those compositions. Bearing in mind that we had an office for which rent had to be found and a staff whose wages had to be paid, we found this new outlet for our music useful.

Then another letter, dated September 28th, arrived from Eddie Kassner, together with an orchestration of a dixieland number entitled 'Distraction', written by Ivor de Bie. The letter here speaks for itself.

Dear Harry,

Please find enclosed one Dixieland orchestration of DISTRACTION by Ivor de Bie. This number has been recorded on the Continent by Django Reinhardt the famous guitarist. I do hope you'll like the work and include it in one of your broadcasts.

I am very much looking forward to your plug on 20th of YOU'RE MADE FOR ME. Jack Leon is doing [it] with vocal on Monday 17th and Eric Winstone gives me a number of dates on it starting on 24th inst.

Please send bill for your arrangement and also the swing number you've promised to write for me, to my office...

Yours Very Sincerely, Eddie R. p.p. Edward Kassner Music Co Ltd.

Eddie Kassner was a very persistent person, as evidenced by the fact that he became the head of a huge publishing and recording company with offices in America – President Records. But I had to decline his request to broadcast 'Distraction'. It wasn't dixieland in style. However, we did become very friendly with Eddie and now and again he would put work our way.

Norrie and I started to write original compositions for publication, placing the pieces with music publishers in return for giving plugs to their tunes. Firstly, we did a number called 'Meander In The Minor', published under the *nom de plume* of Harold Moore. This was followed by 'Dixieland Dilemma'. The dilemma referred to the fact that the melody was based on what could be considered to be the bass part of a theme in dixieland style, together with a counterpoint theme set against the bass line.

The Keith Prowse Company Ltd. wanted an arrangement from us of their copyright of 'American Patrol'. We gladly complied. I was able to write arrangements to suit any size of band. And so it went on with various compositions and arrangements written by us for various publishers and in various styles. This led to our becoming members of the Performing Rights Society. To this day I still get royalties on sales of sheet music for some of my arrangements. That's the way the system of writing, publishing and performing popular music worked at the time.

A Great Team

Broadcasts by the band attracted much favourable comment and we became regular broadcasters. In turn, the broadcasts made us more and more widely known, though occasionally they got cancelled. Once, during the post-war rationing period in 1946, the Minister of Food decided he needed to talk urgently to the public about dried eggs. So we got pushed out, as the *Melody Maker* reported under the headline 'DRIED EGG FOR GOLD!':

> Last minute cancellation of the 11.40 p.m. broadcast on Tuesday (February 5th) of Harry Gold and his Pieces of Eight was due to the talk following the 9 o'clock news by Minister Sir Ben Smith, which

necessitated 15 minutes' dance music being cut, the victim being HARRY GOLD, scheduled for 20 minutes. The extra five minutes was added to Geraldo's preceding 22 minutes. A compensatory airing has been given by the BBC but this cannot take place before the end of the month.

The band personnel was now fixed and the recordings for Parlophone brought us much attention among booking agents. Offers of gigs poured in. We packed halls wherever we went. But both Norrie and I wanted to work in London where we could continue with our writing connections.

I was delighted when a new possibility to get our music heard seemed to present itself. I received a call from the BBC offering a television broadcast from the newly opened studios in Alexandra Palace.[5] But although we performed, the show didn't go out as planned. It was a bitter disappointment. The first thing that went wrong was the result of my having programmed for our broadcast a number that featured Geoff Love and our female singer Jane Lee in a duet. This was always a success when we included it in our performances and I thought it would be ideal for television. But the producer thought otherwise. He called me away, out of earshot of the other musicians and said, "You'll have to take that number out." In amazement, I asked why. "We can't have a coloured fellow and a white girl singing together on television," he said. I couldn't believe what I was hearing and wondered for a moment whether we were actually in London, England. I protested but without success. The number was cut. When I told Geoff and Jane why, Geoff just took it as 'one of those things' in his usual stoical, good-humoured manner. The final blow was that, in the middle of a take, the camera fell down and was put out of action. It was the only camera in use. So

[5] The world's first regular public television service had been started from the BBC station at Alexandra Palace, in Muswell Hill, north London, in November 1936 but transmissions were suspended from September 1939 throughout the war. The service re-started on June 7th 1946 (Ed.)

that was the end of the chance of our being one of the earliest bands to perform on television.[6]

I should point out in passing that the affair of Geoff's and Jane's duet certainly wasn't the only instance of racism that I've come across in my career. There was a lot of prejudice among the owners of digs where the band musicians would stay. I mentioned earlier that, while I was with Oscar Rabin, the fine West Indian saxophonist George Roberts was a member of the reed section for a period. When the band was on tour, Peggy and I would look after George and take him with us when we went to find digs. We would find somewhere and he would stay with us. We shielded him in that way. But I remember one time when five of us – Peggy and me, and three others from the band including George – were looking for digs together. We went to one digs and the landlady looked us over and then said carefully that she had room for only four. She obviously expected George to go and the rest of us to take the digs. But I said, "Well, if there isn't room for the five of us then four of us don't want to stay." And we went elsewhere. People tended to look down on the black musicians. But actually many of them were much better educated than some of the white players.

In 1947 I heard through the Archer Street grapevine that Lew Stone was leaving the Embassy Club, a very plush establishment in Bond Street[7] I thought it would be a great opportunity if I could get the residency there. I knew that the

---

[6] Other bands were soon on the air. A *Radio Times* programme page reproduced in Briggs' *Sound and Vision* lists a half-hour television broadcast as scheduled for 'Harry Roy and His Band with Eric Whitley, Eve Lombard and Harry Kaye' from 3.10 p.m. to 3.30 p.m. on Monday June 10th 1946 (Ed.)

[7] Stone had been resident at the Embassy Club with a medium-sized band, the Novatones, from 1945 to 1947. From 1947 to 1949 he led the theatre orchestra for the musical show 'Annie Get Your Gun' (Ed.)

owner was the brother of a Mr. Abrahams who owned the 400
Club in Leicester Square where Harry Conn was working. I
asked Harry to give me an introduction to Mr. Abrahams and I
took along some of my records for him to hear. Abrahams said
that if I wanted to work for him I would have to sign with an
agency with whom he did all his business. "Go and see Mr.
Arbib of the Anglo-American Agency and tell him I sent you,"
he said. So I went to Mr. Arbib. I found out that the agency
was one of Mr. Abrahams' concerns. Through it he got ten per
cent of the pay of the bandleaders he employed. Arbib put me
in touch with a colleague of his named Cassell Gerard. He
worked at the Embassy Club as a kind of host who would also
dance with unaccompanied ladies.

We got the job at the Embassy Club. The Pieces of Eight
worked there with three violins (including the excellent jazz
violinist George Hurley) and a viola added to the regular line-
up. We played in a kind of demure dixieland style. My father
made uniforms for the band – grey jackets with mauve lapels
and a dinner suit for me to wear. And I remember that
Ambrose, who was working with his band at Ciro's Club at the
time, came in to hear us play.

But there was a problem. It soon became clear that we were
not contracted to the Anglo-American Agency but to Cassell
Gerard who, in the meantime, had left Anglo-American to start
his own organisation. It was a situation fraught with danger for
us because of the looming competition between Cassell Gerard
and his former employer. A struggle developed between the
two agencies and Cassell lost. In a short while I was told by
the Embassy management that we were no longer wanted and
we were replaced by Carl Barriteau under the Anglo-American
banner.[8] Carl was a dear friend. My brother Laurie and I had

---

[8] Reedman Carl Barriteau, born in Trinidad in 1914, had settled in Britain
in 1937. He worked with Ken Johnson for nearly four years and was injured
in the air raid that killed Johnson in March 1941 at the Café de Paris.

known him for years. He was a great cook. He loved to dress up in his chef's outfit when he cooked us meals at his place. And when he organised his big band he invited me to play in it. He was a wonderful musician. Nevertheless, for us in our band, it was a great pity to lose the Embassy job because, up to that time, negotiations had been taking place for an exchange between the Pieces of Eight and the continental European bandleader Bernard Hilda at the Club Les Champs Elysées in Paris. Without our position at the Embassy Club it was a non-starter.

Norrie Paramor and I were worried that the band might split up. After discussing the matter we offered a partnership to my brother and Geoff Love. The partnership developed into a great team. Norrie handled the books and accounts, Laurie the publicity and bookings, Geoff provided ideas on entertainment as well as being a singer and dancer. I remained the front man and continued with the arrangements and the programme planning. This co-operative set-up steered the band to a position as one of the most popular in the country.

Later, our organising activities expanded in other directions too as the band became more and more busy. One day, Norrie Paramor said to me, "We are doing a lot of variety work. It might be a good idea to start a theatrical agency so that we could engage variety and musical acts to work with us as a complete show." Laurie, Geoff and I agreed to the suggestion and we applied for a licence to operate from premises we acquired in Victoria. The company was registered and Airshows Ltd. was born.

Thereafter he was with Lew Stone, Ambrose and various groups during the war, organised his own West Indian Dance Orchestra in 1942, and led bands on ENSA and variety tours before taking over the Embassy Club residency in 1947 (Ed.)

We engaged Bill Sensier[9] to act as manager and my son Leslie, who had left college by then, joined as an assistant. A lady named Alma Arnell, who had set up the Harry Gold Fan Club, became the secretary.

The venture proved successful at first but we soon began to find that we were being squeezed out by the 'big boys' and we eventually abandoned the agency. I remember one of the shows we did, however, which ran for a week at New Brighton, and included the singer-comedian Leon Cortez. He had a fine operatic voice and he was the 'second top' (second from top billing) in this particular show. In his act, he would tell a story with a humorous twist and a double meaning, which was developed all through as he sang his songs. He always finished his act with a bit of by-play with me on stage. I had to give him a bottle of port which he used as a gargle (not in the Irish sense!). He explained to the audience that this was absolutely necessary if he was to be able to hit the high notes. This routine went on each night. On the last show on Saturday, I had added a little brandy to the port without telling him. He took a big swig and turned to me on the stage with an absolutely straight face and declared, "The port seems to have improved. I'll return the compliment in the bar." A nice guy.

Another time, in the same theatre, the manager asked me to include a local comedian in the show we were putting on on the Friday night. According to the manager, this comedian was very popular. Of course, it wouldn't cost us anything to include him so I said yes. He came on and had the audience

---

[9] Bill Sensier, a telephone engineer by trade, was a highly active trade unionist and eventually combined this activity with music promotion. He had organised, on behalf of London branches of the Post Office Engineering Union, the London Philharmonic Orchestra's 'Grand Concert in Aid of Medical Supplies for Russia' on March 9th 1943. Held at the Albert Hall, London, this was the first occasion on which a trade union had sponsored a major music concert for a mass audience. Sensier's story is told in his *A Post Office Engineer* (London: National Communications Union, 1993) (Ed.)

screaming with laughter. I couldn't see what they were laughing at but they really loved him. Since then he has become very famous, especially through television. It was Ken Dodd.

Fighting the BBC

The Pieces of Eight were regularly featured on popular BBC radio shows such as 'Band Parade', 'Let's Make Music', 'Jazz Club' and 'Music While You Work'. In 1948, a little over four years since the band's formation, it was voted among the top bands in Britain in a popularity poll organised by the radio critic of the *Daily Graphic*. But around that time an important change occurred in the broadcasting situation. For us, for a time, it was definitely not a change for the better. Tawny Neilson, who had been ultimately responsible for booking us and providing the break-through into regular broadcasting for the band, left her job with the Dance Band Department. There were some accusations that she had been accepting bribes from bandleaders in exchange for booking their bands for broadcasts.[10] Some well-known leaders were involved and one in particular was alleged to have given her a pricey fur coat. I

---

[10] Kerry Segrave writes, in his *Payola in the Music Industry*, about the official inquiry by Sir Valentine Holmes "to investigate charges of bribery, corruption and favouritism" amongst BBC staff. "Holmes reported the allegations were without solid foundation. None of the BBC staff were named in the report with the exception of Mrs. D. H. Nelson [sic], head of the dance band section. Due to the inquiry, BBC governors severely rebuked Nelson, expressing disapproval of her 'very unwise' acceptance of gifts. Despite acknowledging she was open to severe criticism Holmes added in his report that he didn't think she was influenced in any way as a result of accepting gifts. The BBC issued an order banning staffers from accepting gifts." Segrave cites a report in *Variety*, 'BBC Band Music Dept Head Hit on Payola Rap' (March 26 1947) (Ed.)

can honestly say I never gave her anything unless you take into account the odd bottle of Scotch left at the desk of the Aeolian Hall at Christmas time and the fact that I helped her to arrange the broadcast from the British Embassy grounds in Paris on VE Day.

I did tell Tawny that I would be prepared to give evidence on her behalf but she refused the offer. Rita Williams, who was getting a lot of broadcasts at the time as a solo singer, made a similar offer to Tawny and got a similar response. It should be said that, apart from her good voice and intonation, Rita was a fine music reader and she fully deserved the broadcasting opportunities she received.

Tawny left the BBC and went to New York where she started a recording company. Her position was taken over by an Australian 'new broom' named Jim Davison.[11] He and I didn't get on at all. From my corner, he seemed heavy-handed and rude. I also believe he was intent on getting rid of anyone who had many broadcasts during Tawny Neilson's period of office.

Soon after his arrival at the BBC, he arranged to meet bandleaders who were regularly broadcasting. The meetings were private and individual. At first, I thought that he really wanted to evaluate each individual and become acquainted with each on a friendly basis. Later I found that my first estimate was mistaken. In repeated skirmishes with him, I came to the conclusion that he was a bully. Just my opinion, of course. But suddenly I stopped being booked for broadcasts. I wanted to know why but whenever I phoned his secretary to ask for an appointment he was never available. In the end I had to point

---

[11] Asa Briggs writes, in *Sound and Vision*, that "in May 1948 the Dance Band Department, headed by Mrs. D. Neilson, was closed down – she became a producer – and J. A. Davison, an Australian band-leader, took over as Assistant Head of Variety supervising all broadcasts by dance bands. This was an interesting change which suggested that... 'the dancing years' had gone, perhaps never to return" (Ed.)

out that it was my right to meet him to ask why I was not being offered dates when my programmes were always well planned and the critics' reaction was always favourable. Finally, he condescended to give me a hearing. The time offered for the appointment was 9.00 a.m. I think it was a ploy; it was very early for a meeting. But I agreed. On the morning of the appointment I arrived in his office ten minutes early. He arrived half an hour late but with no apology.

After the opening platitudes we got down to business. "Mr. Gold," he said, "What did you want to see me about?" He knew very well why I had come. I answered, "Mr. Davison, I am wondering why I'm not getting any air time. Have I been dropped for any particular reason?" I thought his reply to that was offensive: "Why do you think you're entitled to broadcast time more than anyone else?" I knew I had a battle on my hands. In such situations, we humans seem to gather mental strength. My answer was, "On the basis of the popularity of my band with the listening public as well as the band's theatrical and dance hall audiences." I went on, "I'm not greedy and I don't think I'm more important than anyone else, but I think I'm entitled to a reasonable slice of the cake." That shook him. He thought for a few seconds and then gave me two dates for broadcasts. I thanked him, and had got out of my chair ready to leave when he said, "See ya, Harry!", shaking my hand and surprising me more than somewhat by the use of my forename. But it wasn't the victory I at first thought.

That became clear some months later. Because we were on tour at times, we made it a habit to send a month's availability schedule in advance to the BBC. That was my brother's responsibility. He had worked out a system which showed not only dates when we were available but also specific times. It also showed clearly when we were not available. Laurie was meticulous about this. I realised what was in the wind when two dates came through on days that our schedule clearly showed as not available. We had to decline. For a long period, there were no broadcasts offered. I checked that the availability lists had been sent to the BBC to make sure that we had kept them properly informed. We had. So I realised something was wrong. I made another phone call to Jim and got the usual runaround. Then I told his secretary I was going to contact the Head of Light Music. That brought the desired response. A meeting with Davison was hastily arranged. You see, I had already tested his mettle and I knew that, faced with unavoidable and unwanted consequences, he would give in.

Laurie had kept file copies of all the schedules he had sent to Jim Davison's office. I arrived at the meeting armed with a folder containing the copies. The usual banalities over I opened the discussion by asking, "Why am I not getting any dates?" He replied, "You were offered two and you turned them down." So, with a self-satisfied smile, I produced the sheaf of 'goodies' Laurie had supplied and pointed out that Davison's office had known very well that we wouldn't be available on the dates offered. Then he played his master stroke. He buzzed down to his secretary and asked her to find in her files our availability list for the period in question. He was told they had "been mislaid". In faked anger, he turned to me and said, "That makes me see red," and then he added, "Are you a red?" He waited for the effect of his words. It was a time when people on the left were being victimised because of the Cold War fears of communism. I could see which way the wind was blowing so I replied, "Mr. Davison, I'm under the impression that I'm here to talk about broadcasts, not about politics." He had the grace to apologise.

The final clash concerned a broadcast we had been offered while we were in Weston-super-Mare for a summer season. As the broadcast would take place in the morning in London, I knew we could make the journey there by train and get back to Weston by air in time for our evening show. I hired a small

Playing farewell to Australian bandleader Graeme Bell, leaving London for Australia in 1948 after his first extended playing visit to the UK. Bell was an important pioneer in the popularisation of traditional jazz in Britain. Behind me are Geoff Love (trombone), Cyril Ellis (trumpet) and drummer Eric Galloway. The clarinettist on the far right is Bruce Turner. On his right is Carlo Krahmer, co-founder of Esquire Records, for which Bell recorded.

The Pieces of Eight having fun at Weston-Super-Mare, 1949. Left to right: Laurie Gold, HG, Betty Taylor, Geoff Hawkins, Johnny Wise, Freddie Tomasso, Geoff Love, Ernie Tomasso, Norrie Paramor (Weston-Super-Mare *Gazette* photo).

The Pieces of Eight at the Jazz Jamboree, Kilburn, late 1940s. Left to right: Norrie Paramor, Cyril Ellis, Bert Weedon, Geoff Love, HG, Eric Galloway, Ralph Bruce, Laurie Gold, Bill Haines. My father made these uniforms (grey with mauve lapels) for our Embassy Club engagement.

Club party, probably 1949. Left to right at the table: Geoff Love, Joan Paramor, Norrie Paramor and Peggy Gold. BBC Jazz Club producer Mark White is next to me on the right.

Jon Clarke singing with the Pieces of Eight. Early 1950s.

At Morecambe with Peggy and 'Genevieve', 1953 (photo courtesy of *The Visitor*, Morecambe).

Photographer Chris Hayes decided he just couldn't keep up with the Pieces of Eight schedule. Sympathising are Al Doniger, Ernie Tomasso, Danny Craig and me. Liverpool, February 1953, after the band's dash by air from Cork (photo courtesy of Chris Hayes).

The Pieces of Eight, c.1953. Left to right: Betty Taylor, Jimmy McKnight, Ted Darrah, Freddie Tomasso, HG, Ernie Tomasso, Tony Lytton, Laurie Gold, unknown, Jimmy Day.

Left to right: jazz accordionist and bandleader Tito Burns, sports writer Noel Whitcombe, singer Terry Devon, Peggy Gold, HG, Peggy Coles, trumpeter Jack Coles. 1950s.

That's entertainment! Doing the ventriloquist act, Cayton Bay Holiday Camp, Scarborough, late 1950s.

After-hours birthday party at the Yorkshire Grey, Clerkenwell, 1980. My brother Laurie and Bob Layzell are on the left.

Sitting in with American bandleader Turk Murphy at his Club 'Earthquake McGoon's', San Francisco, c.1981 (photo by Gary Schroeder, courtesy of San Francisco Traditional Jazz Foundation).

That's entertainment, too! Keith Nichols playing trombone with his foot during the Pieces of Eight tour of East Germany, September 1984.

A Pieces of Eight line-up from the early 1980s. Left to right: Roy Crimmins, Gerry Ingram, Al Wynette, Bob Layzell, Stan Daly, HG, Martin Litton (photo by Bernard Long).

Palast der Republik

Harry Gold And His Pieces Of Eight

Besetzung
Harry Gold (ts, bss)
Al Wynette (tp)
Roy Crimmins (tb)
Bob Layzell (cl, ts)
Keith Nichols (p)
Pete Corrigan (b)
Stan Daly (dr)

Programme for the second East Germany tour, February 1985. In the picture, Keith Nichols is on trombone and Austin Malcolm on piano; others as indicated.

Blending lower registers with John Barnes at the 100 Club, London, March 1989 (photo by Peter Symes).

Still side by side! With Laurie (photo by Bernard Long).

Accepting the Freedom of the City of London, at the Guildhall, 1988, with Peggy, our son Andrew and Mary, our neighbour in Theobalds Road.

Just another couple of queries, Harry.' Hard at work on this book with my editor, North London, May 1999.

Musicians' Union celebration of my more than 70 years in the music business, Clerkenwell Festival, London, July 1999. On the left, Horace Trubridge, MU Central London Secretary. On the right, Dennis Scard, MU General Secretary, tries out my presentation tankard for size.

Receiving the BT British Jazz Award, May 1997. Ken Booth (BT) on the left, jazz critic Benny Green on the right (photo by Jim Simpson).

plane to bring us back. But I was informed later that it would be dark for the landing and, unfortunately, the local airport had no landing lights. My plan for getting to London and back would not work. The contracts for the broadcast had been signed and so I had to tell Jim the situation. He blew his top. He said, "You guys want to eat the cake and keep it." I offered to pay for the producer to come to Bristol and do the broadcast from the studio there. Davison turned that down, but he arranged for a local producer and studio balancer to be on hand at the Bristol studio. They turned out to be very good and the situation, fraught with danger, was saved.

Eventually Mr. Davison left the BBC. He didn't last as long there as Tawny.

New Management

As far as the band's live engagements were concerned a further change of direction was made possible when a letter came from someone named Lewis Buckley. He was an agent who was completely unknown to me at the time but he proved to be a real go-getter. He had written from an address in Southport in Lancashire. He proposed to offer his complete efforts provided that we signed a contract making him our sole agent. For his services he would have ten per cent of all fees received for our engagements.

In principle it meant that offers from any other source apart from Lewis would have to be handed over to him. We had a lengthy meeting with him in which we pointed out that broadcasts could not be part of the agreement. All the broadcast offers we received were the result of previous action on our part. In any case, the BBC payments were not all that lucrative and we could not pay commission on those engagements.

He was a very shrewd man and saw our point of view immediately. The contract was signed, with an option for either side to cancel after a year's trial. Making the agreement with Lewis proved to be the best thing we could have done. The only drawback was that we worked seven days a week (sometimes playing a double concert on Sundays) without having a break. It became apparent that we would all suffer in health if we continued at that pace.

One of the Sunday double concerts, on September 5th 1948, was a real 'red letter day'. The band was contracted by top agents, Bernard Delfort and Ed W. Jones, for a double concert at the De Montfort Hall, Leicester, to support Hoagy Carmichael. In our first set, before Hoagy came on, we played pieces such as 'High Society', 'Tiger Rag', 'Jazz Me Blues', 'Hawaiian War Chant' and 'At the Jazz Band Ball' and Geoff Love and our female singer Jane Lee did several feature numbers. It was a typical set but I decided that, as a tribute to Hoagy, the last number we played before I introduced him would be his composition 'Riverboat Shuffle'. His entrance was greeted with cheers and tremendous applause and, when he was able to speak, his first words were, "Great band. It's a long time since I heard that back-beat stuff." Afterwards, he gave me an autographed photo.

We were beginning to get more gigs than the amount of work available in the arranging department allowed time for. So this was the start of another change of direction. We decided to emphasise the band more and cut back on the arranging side. Apart from one-offs such as the Hoagy Carmichael concert, all the dates at that time were dance dates, so we needed a singer of popular tunes of the day. That meant engaging anyone available for a specific date. Sometimes it would be Marie Benson, who sang on the air with many bands. At other times we hired Jo Lennard (a lovely jazz singer), Benny Lee (who later became a comedian in the variety series 'Pettycoat Lane' broadcast live from the People's Palace in the East End) and several others from the pool. Although the war had ended, it was still difficult to have permanent musicians and singers.

Around that time, I don't remember exactly when, we were offered – completely out of the blue – a fortnight's engagement at Seaburn Hall, Sunderland and we needed a vocalist for the two weeks. We engaged, on recommendation, Frances Tanner, whom we didn't know. She told us that she would not be able to appear for the first night because of a previous engagement but she would be able to do the rest of the fortnight. She said, "Don't worry about that. It can be covered by my sister Stella. She's very good and we often work together as a double act." We kept quiet to the management about the change because they had been told that the name of the singer would be Frances Tanner and they had printed posters and publicity on that basis.

At the end of the first night I pointed out to Norrie, Geoff and Laurie that at the next day's performance by the band, when Frances appeared as the singer, it would be obvious that the management had been deceived. So we had better come clean immediately. They not only agreed but said, "Why don't we hire them both?" Someone added, "Stella is a good singer and has a fine personality. Frances must be equally good and, if they work as a double act, they could be an asset." And so it proved. They were excellent in variety shows, during which they used material from their own act. They stayed with us for a while. But soon they decided that they really wanted to work together in their own act as a team. So they went to work for ENSA and eventually broke through into opportunities in theatre, films and television.

After the end of the job at the Embassy Club, Ralph Bruce had left the band, which meant finding another clarinet player. An advert and news item in the *Melody Maker* brought a phone call from a clarinettist named Ernie Tomasso who came from

Leeds.[12] He said he would send a record. When it arrived, I was delighted to hear what sounded like an American clarinet player. It was Ernie, and of course we engaged him straight away, while noting the ability of the trumpet player on the record. It turned out to be Ernie's brother Freddie.

Cyril Ellis was now a regular member of the Pieces and was proving to be an asset. We needed a vocalist and had engaged, first of all, Jane Lee, whom I mentioned earlier. She stayed with us for a long time until Cyril Ellis started to court her. In the fullness of time Cyril and Jane married and Jane wanted to leave to build a home. That meant another round of auditions.

Auditioning is a boring way of spending time but when needs must the devil drives, so we spent all day in a studio listening to females squawking and screeching in what was supposed to be singing. Then, suddenly a shaft of light! Two ladies auditioned for us in quick succession and we knew our troubles were over. The first singer was Betty Driver, who has since become an actress. The other was Betty Taylor, whom we finally chose because of her range of contralto going into mezzo soprano. Soon after Jane had left, Cyril Ellis followed her. Remembering the trumpet player on Ernie Tomasso's record, we contacted Freddie and he joined the band in place of Cyril.[13]

Lewis Buckley and the four partners met to resolve the excessive work situation and we came to the conclusion that we should have a break from touring every six weeks. It was also agreed that every year the band should take a fortnight's holiday with all members being paid for the two weeks. New

---

[12] Tomasso, born in Leeds in 1912, had led the RAF Rhythm Kings during the war and then his own band in Morecambe in 1946-7. He worked mainly with Harry Gold until 1953. In the mid-1950s he co-led the Tomasso Brothers' Band with his brother Freddie (Ed.)

[13] Freddie was with the Pieces of Eight from January 1949 until November 1952, when he joined Harry Roy's band (Ed.)

contracts were prepared to include the new conditions and a copy was sent to Mr. Dambman, who was then the Musicians' Union's General Secretary, for union approval. Not only was approval given but some of the clauses we had devised were embodied in a union standard touring contract.

Paris Blues

At a band meeting, we agreed on the first holiday period. It was set for the first two weeks in August. That holiday turned out to be a disaster for Peggy and me. I had made up my mind that part of it should be spent in Luxembourg. At that time I was also musical director for Radio Luxembourg and I was hoping to meet up with some of my professional contacts there. I had done a lot of arrangements for a singer named Lee Lawrence who broadcast on Radio Luxembourg. The listeners seemed to like the music a great deal. So I had become actively involved with the radio station and the Pieces of Eight made records for transmission via Radio Luxembourg.

Peggy and I travelled on the Night Ferry (the night version of the Golden Arrow express train) which had provision for sleeping berths. The plan was to meet Norrie, Geoff, Laurie and Ernie Tomasso in Paris. We would have three days there with them and then they would go their separate ways for the rest of the holiday. When Peggy and I woke we were nearing Paris. Our breakfast was taken in the train's restaurant car and we arrived at nine o'clock in the morning, too early to meet up with Norrie, Geoff, Laurie and Ernie, who had travelled earlier.

Peggy had never been to Paris, so I suggested we should see some sights before going to the hotel where we were to meet the others. We travelled by Metro and as it was very hot I took off my jacket, holding it over my arm. After seeing the Eiffel

Tower we retraced our steps. Then I discovered that my wallet had disappeared with all my French money and valuable vouchers. We went to the police, then to the British Embassy for help. What a waste of time that proved to be! All the Consul was prepared to do was provide us with third class fare home and at the same time hold our passports as security for a loan to cover our living expenses in Paris.

I was in a panic. It wasn't very long after the end of the war. Money was still strictly controlled and it was necessary to apply to the Bank of England for some money to be sent abroad, and the application had to be vetted. I was told that I would have to wait a week for the result of the vetting process. That meant being in Paris without any means of financial support.

Off we went to meet the lads at the Hôtel Gare du Nord. By that time they were awake, had had breakfast and were awaiting our arrival. After the expected welcome, I gave the sad news. Of course, they turned up trumps, each of them giving us some money as a standby. Then I went to see the Paris representative of the *Melody Maker* and told him my predicament. He said, "The editor owes me some money. I'll phone him and ask if I could lend you 10,000 francs on top of what is owing to me from the *Melody Maker*. You could pay the editor when you get back to London."

The editor was Pat Brand. He and I were very good friends and as soon as the call was connected the phone was handed to me so that I could speak to Pat direct. I explained the situation and Pat said, "Of course. No problem." He immediately authorised the loan which meant that Peggy and I had enough money while waiting for the Bank of England to sanction the transfer of funds from England. Confirmation came the same week but it was too late for us to go to Luxembourg and have our holiday. Instead, we went to Deauville where the Roy Fox band had played. We went to the Casino for a gamble at the 'wheel'. As I mentioned earlier, Deauville Casino had two sections. There was one for the rich and the other for the rest, which is where we went, losing a franc at a time. Big deal!

The final disastrous end to our holiday occurred after Peggy had eaten some mussels. She had to stay in bed with severe stomach pains which lasted three days.

Arriving home, we found a letter awaiting us. It had been sent by a lady who worked in an outfitters' store in Paris. She wrote that she had found my wallet. She wanted to know what she should do. I wrote asking her to deliver it to John Arslanian's parents who lived in Paris. I also contacted them and asked them to give the lady ten per cent of what was in the wallet. What made me really angry was that the finder explained in her letter that she had taken the wallet to the Embassy and had been given short shrift. Even worse, she had been there before I had, so I could have got the wallet back when I called there if the Embassy had taken it in.

I wrote to the Ambassador pointing out that the Embassy was supposed to help British citizens in difficult situations. After a delay of three weeks, a letter of sincere apology arrived. I assume the Ambassador had investigated the matter.

Weston

Touring continued until, during 1949, Lewis Buckley asked if we were interested in a summer season at Weston-super-Mare playing for dancing in the Winter Gardens. It sounded like a good idea. It would be a relief from the incessant travelling. We could also take advantage of the opportunity to be with our families and enjoy the seaside and sun. We found places for the youngsters in the local schools in Weston and settled down to a working holiday. The personnel was the same as the band had had for touring: Norrie Paramor on piano; Geoff Love on trombone; Ernie and Freddie Tomasso on clarinet and trumpet, respectively; my brother Laurie on tenor sax and clarinet; Johnny Wise (drums); Geoff Hawkins (double bass) and Betty Taylor (vocals). Of course, I made up the full complement.

Although we were playing for dancing, the style (apart from for waltzes and tangos) was dixieland. It proved to be very successful. But I soon found that the fans always wanted the same tunes, which was a bit of a bore. On Thursday nights, the management organised an 'Old Tyme Night' and engaged a different band for the occasion. Although that freed us on Thursdays from appearing as usual, we didn't get the night off. We were asked to play a concert every Thursday at the open air bandstand which, on other nights, was usually occupied by a military band. I thought it would be a good opportunity to play a complete jazz programme every Thursday night. I arranged to have leaflets placed on the seats so that people could write down their requests. I thought we could really vary the programme that way taking account of audience preferences. But week after week the requests were predictably the same. You can't win!

While we were in Weston there was a drive to enlist blood donors. I volunteered and suggested to the members of the band that they should do the same. They all agreed and we got terrific publicity in the local papers as a result. I continued to be a regular donor until the age of 65 when I was told that I would not be needed for this any more. It was a disappointment not to be able to continue to give blood because I always felt very well after a donation. It was an exhilarating experience, but I can't explain why.

One of the doctors at Weston became very friendly and later started his own surgery in South London. He became very helpful in enabling us to cope with our tiring travel routines. My friend was able to supply us with little yellow pills which gave a lift up and kept us going. However, we also found that we couldn't sleep with such a pace of life. The touring life meant that we had to be up and living on energy but also we had to be down and able to rest. So he gave us other capsules that knocked us out. I can see how easy it can be to get on to harder drugs. But we didn't.

There was one incident involving that doctor and me that was serious at the time but later became a joke. While we were doing a series of one-night stands I noticed blood stains on my underpants and felt itching in the lower regions. I asked the doctor to examine me. His first question was, "Have you ever had gonorrhoea?" When I said I hadn't he asked if I was in pain, to which the reply was, "No. Positively not." He couldn't give an opinion there and then but he asked where I was going. I told him we were playing Edinburgh Empire for a week and he said, "If you get any pain, phone me and I'll come wherever you may be."

A couple of days later, I told Laurie who was staying in the same hotel. He said, "Let's have a look." I lowered my pants and he stared for a few moments. Then he began to laugh hysterically. I thought he had gone mad. "What's the joke," I demanded. "Harry, you've got crab lice," he said. I was horror struck. I'd never heard of the little sods. I thought crabs were a kind of fish with claws, not blood-sucking insects. You can see that Denny Dennis wasn't the only naive person in the world. What's more, I had been to a doctor who was totally unaware of my condition. Laurie explained what they were and how people can get them. I couldn't understand how I had managed to get a full complement without even trying.

The first thing, of course, was to get rid of them. Laurie said, "Go to a chemist and ask for blue unction. Come back here, cut all the hair away, put a large quantity of the ointment on the affected part and have a bath." The idea of 'unction' (in the extreme) made me think about going to priests! I didn't mention it. After all, it wasn't much good going to a doctor either, was it?

With a mind-blowing thought I realised how I had collected the loathsome little things. Three members of the band tended to sleep in the coach instead of staying in a hotel, even though they all received a regular hotel allowance. I had a camp bed next to the driver's seat so that I could rest on overnight journeys and also give Taffy our driver a break. It seems that one of them must have been using my bed and blanket. I never found out who. I couldn't ask the question directly, could I? When we got back to London, I went to see the doctor. I told him what had happened and guess what! He fell about laughing.

7.

THE GUYS IN THE BAND

Geoff Love worked with the Pieces of Eight for several years and was a much valued partner with Norrie, Laurie and me. We made a good team. But one day in 1949 Geoff said to me, "I've bad news for you." I asked him what was wrong and he said, "I'm very sorry to have to tell you that I have to leave the band. I've had a wonderful time and we've been great friends but the family is growing up and they need me." I knew how he felt as sometimes I was having similar thoughts. I wished him luck. Of course, he went on to great success with his own projects.

After Geoff left, various trombonists worked with the band. Bobby Mickleburgh, who also played trumpet, was among them. Ted Darrah joined for a time after working with Joe Loss. And there was Norman Cave.[1] Norman was a bit of a character. He arrived late one night at a hall in Grimsby. He had solemnly promised that he would be there for the start of the band's performance. But, travelling from London, he hadn't arrived when we went on to the stand and were about to

---

[1] Norman Cave, who came from Liverpool, had worked with Freddy Randall before joining Harry's band for a year from the autumn of 1952. After leaving the Pieces of Eight he rejoined Randall, led his own band and worked with Sid Phillips and many other groups. In the late 1970s he worked mainly as a solo pianist or accompanist for singers and later moved to California where he continued to work both as a pianist and a trombonist. The widely-experienced Bobby Mickleburgh worked with the Pieces of Eight at the end of the 1950s. Later he was a key member of the Temperance Seven traditional jazz band for many years (Ed.)

start. We decided that we would have to play without a trombone.

I was about to beat in the first number when he walked in with his suitcase and trombone, full of apologies. He said he had got on the wrong train by mistake. We delayed starting so as to give him time to wash and change. He unpacked and found that he had left his black shoes behind. It was impossible to find shoes at such short notice, but the manager came up with a pair of wellington boots. Norman had to wear them under his trousers. I was tempted to mark them 'left' and 'right' to make sure nothing else went wrong. But I resisted the urge.

Norman was a huge fellow with a nose that would have been suitable for a heavyweight boxer's face, but he wasn't a fighter. He was quite a gentle person and never seemed to lose his cool. But he could be tough when necessary. One time we were travelling in the band coach through London and had stopped to drop Laurie off to go to the office, which was then in Victoria. We were just about to drive off again when Taffy our driver looked in his mirror and said, "Laurie's having a fight out there." A big fellow had come up to him and was trying to take some money from him. Laurie was doing his best to resist.

Norman took one look at the situation and, without a word, bounded out of the coach. He ran straight past Laurie, lifted the other man up in the air and then dropped him in a crumpled heap on the ground. Some policemen came up, having watched Laurie's fight with his attacker without intervening. Now they wanted an explanation from Norman. The other man claimed Norman had made an entirely unprovoked attack on him. Eventually, it was possible to convince them what the rights and wrongs were. If they had been interested earlier in what was happening perhaps Norman wouldn't have needed to intervene.

He was a fine trombone player but I couldn't understand how it was that now and again he seemed to get under the influence of alcohol, not in the pub but on the bandstand while we were playing. One night I caught him out. I happened to turn in his direction and saw him with a straw in his mouth, sucking away at something inside his jacket. He had a bottle tucked away in his inside pocket. I'm sorry to say that eventually he had to go.

Looking for a Laugh

The never-ending touring continued but it was fun. The chaps were always looking for a laugh which made for a happy band. Of course, the personnel changed as the years went by. For example, we had a succession of drummers. One was Eric Galloway, who claimed he was a nephew of the owner of the Galloway's Cough Syrup business. I remember a trip to Wales soon after he joined the band. Eric arrived at my house with his drum kit and pedal tympani. He wanted me to take the whole lot by car to Paddington Station to catch a train to Milford Haven, where the band had an engagement. We had decided not to travel by coach because of the long distance. But there was no way I could take Eric, the drum kit, his clothing case, the tymp and myself in a two-seater sports car. If he had told me in advance about the tymp, I would have told him to leave it at home. In the end I had to leave it at my place, which took up extra time. We reached the station in time for me to park the car and find our reserved compartment. But the episode taught me a little about Eric's personality and I got a fuller knowledge during our visit to Wales.

We had been booked into a hotel which had a haunted room. At least that was the owner's story. The door of the haunted room was sealed. When Eric heard about the reputed haunting he suggested that we should hold a seance to see if we could contact the ghost. By then I had become a convinced spiritualist (as I still am today) but when Eric suggested the seance I couldn't resist the urge to lumber him.

I thought about it for a long time and eventually arrived at a plan. I had a word privately with the others and arranged that Betty should invite Eric to go to the cinema with her while the rest of us would go shopping for essential articles. These included a thick and heavy chain, some elastic, a half dozen balloons, a length of 5 amp electric flex and a push button bell switch.

While Eric and Betty were in the cinema, the rest of us went to work fixing the room. The first thing to be done was to remove the light switch cover near the door and attach the flex to each side of the live and neutral terminals. The switch cap was then replaced and the flex drawn around the room to a place where I intended to sit. The other end of the flex was attached to the bell push which was placed near my foot position. That made it possible for the light to be switched on and off by my foot even though the light had been switched off at the door.

The chain was attached to the elastic which was also arranged near my foot position. If the elastic was drawn across the floor, the chain would move and make a sound, as though someone or something was moving while wearing chains (or so I hoped). The balloons were blown up and sealed with paper clips. With everything prepared, we waited for the return of Eric and Betty.

When they had arrived and we were all seated and the 'seance' was about to begin, I asked someone to switch the light off. "Now, empty your minds of all thought," I said. There was a minute or two of complete silence. Then I pressed the bell push and on came the light. "How could that happen?" came the chorus from the participants. "Perhaps the switch is faulty," I said. "Eric, would you try to see if it's all right?" He got up, switched the light on and off and declared, "No, it seems OK." He returned to the table and, after a few more tricks with the light, came the chain act. I must say that the conspirators did a fine job of acting when the chain was drawn back and forth on the elastic.

The final devastating blow came with the release of the balloons, one by one. One of them swerved from side to side across the room accompanied by shouts of alarm from Eric. Eventually the peals of laughter from the rest of us made him realise that the whole thing had been faked. He wasn't pleased. Poor Eric was very gullible and didn't think things out very well. The episode was funny at the time but now, in the light of my beliefs, I wish it hadn't happened. I am convinced that there is a spirit world but we were making fun of the idea at Eric's expense.

Tony Lytton was another drummer who worked with us for some time. He had precise rhythm, a relaxed style and was fine for dixieland music. He had been working at the Café de Paris when I hired him – the club was rebuilt after the war to look just as it had been in the years before the bomb destroyed it. I went to hear Tony there and asked him to join. Another drummer, Merton Kaufman, who had sat in with the band occasionally, also worked with us. But at the end of 1952, we had to change the drummer again and advertised in the *Melody Maker* to say we would be holding auditions for a replacement in Mac's Club, in Great Windmill Street, adjoining Archer Street.

We were surprised at the large number of applicants who turned up for the audition. Just before it started, Laurie called me aside and whispered, "Watch out for a red-headed Scot who has just returned from Kenya. He's very good. His name is Danny Craig." All auditions are very boring and this one was no exception until a red-headed Scot sat down at his kit and started to play. It was clear he was streets ahead of the others. I went up to him, sure that we had found our man, and said, "OK Danny, thanks. I'll talk to you later."

I had 'boobed' in a big way. That drummer wasn't Danny Craig but a chap called Joe Gibbons. Danny arrived a little later and I found it difficult to choose between the two. In the meantime Joe had left, taking it for granted that he was not going to get the job. We engaged Danny but tried to find Joe's address to keep for future use. In fact, Joe did join the band later. He told me then that he thought the rehearsal had been fixed when he heard me say, "OK Danny".

Danny Craig was a real find.[2] Unfortunately, he insisted on travelling in his own car with his girl friend (Maxine Russell), a singer who also joined the band. On one of these journeys they had a violent row and parted company. After a while Norman Cave noticed that Maxine was unattached and started to date her. Danny gave us an ultimatum. He said, "It's either her or me." We had no choice and had to let her go. There were several good singers around but only one Danny Craig. Danny had a long stay with us, working with the Pieces of Eight until 1955.

The band personnel might change but the travelling schedule went on. On one occasion we took a long train journey to Haverfordwest in Wales to play for an annual ball. I did something that no doubt many others have wanted to do. I pulled the communication cord and stopped the train. In this case it wasn't devilment, it was sheer necessity. Here is how it happened. The train had stopped at Haverfordwest station and,

---

[2] Danny Craig (Craigie), from Dundee, worked with Harry from December 1952 until May 1955. Immediately before joining the Pieces of Eight he had worked in Kenya with his own band and, before that, with Oscar Rabin, Duncan Whyte, Harry Roy and Harry Parry, among others. After leaving the Pieces, he played with Harry Hayes, Ambrose, Sandy Brown and others, and was with pianist Dill Jones' trio from 1957 to 1960. In the 1960s he freelanced extensively (Ed.).

as usual, Laurie got out first to find a barrow for the instruments and luggage, while I stayed behind to make sure that nothing had been left on the train. A porter shut the carriage door just as I was about to leave the train. Unfortunately, the door handle was on the outside and the window was closed. It would not open and the guard blew his whistle, signalling the driver to start. I was panic stricken. I didn't know how far the next station was and I had to get back to join the others. So I pulled the cord. It took some minutes for the train to stop in the middle of nowhere.

Along came the guard to investigate the reason for the stoppage and discover the culprit – the delinquent who had stopped the train. With my best George Washington honesty, I owned up. He started to attack me verbally but I told him, "The porter closed the door and I couldn't get it open because the window was faulty." I also said that I had a contract to appear at Haverfordwest and that unless arrangements were made to get me there in time for my playing engagement I would sue the railway. To my astonishment, the train made an unscheduled stop at a small station and, on arriving, there was a car waiting to take me to Haverfordwest. I don't know how it was done. Trains were not fitted with radios in those days.

The guard on the train had taken my name and address (the business address) and a couple of months later we were visited in the office by two plainclothes railway policemen who threatened to summons me for wrongfully pulling the communication cord. After I made a counter threat to sue the railway, it was agreed by both sides to drop the matter.

On another journey, it was Laurie who suffered. We were about to take our seats on a train bound for the north of England. As usual Laurie looked after the loading of the instruments. He organised a porter and a large truck to get them in to the luggage compartment at the end of the train. As the final instrument was loaded the guard blew the whistle.

Laurie thought he had better get aboard the luggage van and then walk through the train to join the rest of us in our compartment. Unfortunately, the door leading to the rest of the train was locked and the first stop was miles away at Crewe. Poor Laurie had to stand and occasionally sit on a case until the train stopped. He wasn't pleased. In fact he was livid, having been in the luggage van for two hours without a drink and unable to relieve himself. "Didn't any of you wonder where I was?" he said. Of course, we thought he had found a seat somewhere else. We couldn't have known he was marooned in the luggage van. In any case, in the circumstances we couldn't have helped.

A Bus, Its Driver and the Road

Although some of our journeys were travelled by train during the time that Geoff Love was a member of the band, most were made by means of a coach hired from a firm named Valliant. The driver (always the same one) was a Welshman who insisted on being called Taffy. He was an excellent driver but, like so many who have to drive continually for a living, he sometimes fell foul of bad road conditions, always in winter.

One such occasion occurred on returning from a gig on the south coast. The road was icy and, in spite of Taffy's careful driving, we went into a massive skid by the Devil's Punch Bowl in Surrey and found ourselves perilously perched on the edge of a soft drop. We all got out to inspect the situation and found that the coach could not be moved. So we stood at the roadside waving at the passing traffic to try to get a lift. Success came after a freezing hour's wait when an empty lorry pulled up. The driver offered his help and we were able to return to London with our instruments, cold but unharmed.

Another engagement in mid-winter was at a ballroom in a small town near Ulverston in Cumberland. On the way there we again hit snow – but snow in those parts can reach mountainous heights and this was no exception. Taffy did a wonderful job of steering out of skids, particularly on the descending gradients, one in seven or more. The coach slithered all over the roads. We finally arrived in the town where we were to play, only to discover that we couldn't get near the hall for snowdrifts. We had to leave the coach and walk to the hall through the snow carrying our instruments in our arms.

Then, inside the hall, came the shock. Our contract had not been for a fixed fee but for a share of the door takings, split on a 60%/40% basis. Because of the appalling weather, only seven people had turned up. The proprietor wanted to cancel the gig and refund the attendees' money. Norrie, Laurie and I had a quick discussion. We decided that we would play anyway for the seven customers who had travelled in the same conditions we had. The show would go on. They had turned out as we had and in those circumstances we thought that they should get value for their money. In any case, we were snowed in and would have to stay the night there. So we thought we should make the best of the situation and have a party. I'm not sure who were the most pissed in the end but we all had a ball. It's no use 'crying over spilt milk'.

While we were on another journey in one of Valliant's coaches, Taffy the driver told me that British European Airways was selling off their one-and-a-half-deck coaches at auction. He said, "Would you be interested in bidding for one?" I said I would be and asked him to find out when the auction would take place. He phoned later with the information but, at the same time, he suggested, "Why don't we go there to have a look at the coaches and make an offer before the auction takes place?" I replied, "Before that I want to know who will drive the coach, if I buy one." He said, "I will, if you want me." So we made an appointment to view. We wandered around the huge open space where the coaches were parked, with Taffy examining them and me totally ignorant of what he was looking for. Soon, Taffy came up, saying, "Mr. Gold, I've found a really good one. I suggest you offer £250 for it." I thought that was a ridiculously low price to suggest, but he was adamant. Surprisingly, the offer was accepted.

Taffy drove the coach to central London, parking in John Street, close to where I lived in Theobalds Road. We now had our own means of band transport which proved to be very useful. First of all, the vehicle had to be painted. The letters 'BEA' stood out for all to see. We decided to keep the original dark blue paint but it needed a thorough clean-up. Then we had the words 'HARRY GOLD AND HIS PIECES OF EIGHT' put on the sides and on the back of the enormous boot which would hold all our instruments, our music library, luggage and uniforms. It was also agreed that we would make John Street the regular pick-up point for the coach. In fact, we kept it parked there.

Once the coach was in use, a remarkable phenomenon could be noticed. When we had travelled by train, everyone would arrive at the platform at least ten minutes before departure time. This situation continued for a short while after we started to use our own coach but, gradually, one or another of the band members would drift in at exactly the appointed time; then gradually the delay would increase and finally someone would usually be ten minutes or so late for departure. When this was pointed out to the guys, punctuality would return for a time and then there would be a reversion to lateness. The assumption, of course, was that we wouldn't leave without the latecomer(s). Taffy complained, with justification. He said that if we left for a destination at a later time than agreed it put a severe strain on him as driver. The result of all this was that we were forced to set the starting time earlier than necessary to make up for those who couldn't conform to the schedule. It wasn't fair to those who did keep to time but there was no alternative. Those who came late always had a feasible excuse of a kind that never seemed to be needed when travelling by train.

Still, having the coach was an excellent improvement and, of course, the publicity as we traversed the country's lanes and towns was an added bonus. And Taffy was a gem. He not only serviced the coach – he said he wanted to be sure it was done properly – but he also helped the 'roadie'. Having a road manager to look after the instruments – loading them on and off the coach, setting up the stand and sometimes setting the instruments out on it – had become an absolute necessity to cope with our busy touring schedules.

When we did long journeys that involved a return to base the same night, it was our practice to drop the members near their homes, leaving me until last, because the coach would be parked near my house. On one such return, the coach having stopped opposite my front door, the roadie (I'll call him Fred for reasons to be seen) helped me across the road with my bag and instruments. When we reached the other side, a voice coming from the adjacent mews shouted Fred's surname (which I'm not at liberty to mention). I ignored the shouting and opened the front door, and we went up to the floor level of my flat. The owner of the voice still followed, calling the name. I had just opened the door of the flat and put my things inside when a man appeared and claimed to be a detective sergeant. He asked what we were doing. He obviously had the idea that we were shifting stolen property. But I said, "This is private property and you have no right here unless you have a warrant. I've just put my personal property into my flat," and I insisted that he should leave.

"I want you," he told Fred. "You're coming with me." I told him Fred was working for me and that if he took Fred to the police station I would come along as well. So we went to the station where I saw the desk sergeant (who knew who I was) and told him that Fred was working for me and had just been helping to bring my things in. "What's the charge?" I asked. "He's done nothing wrong. I want him released immediately." The detective told the sergeant that Fred was a criminal and that he had been in prison. I was angry at that comment in my presence and I told him, "You have no right to mention that in my hearing." The sergeant agreed. "He is free to go," he said. "He is not being charged." On the way out I said to Fred, "I don't want to know what you did. Just do your job and don't worry." He was grateful.

There is a sequel. Fred stayed a long time with us and kept his nose clean. He and Taffy worked as a team, even to the point of unpacking the instruments and setting up the stage. But then we had a fortnight at Green's Playhouse in Glasgow, which meant that their services were not required for that time. So they enjoyed themselves for the two weeks. After we had finished the last Saturday night session of the engagement, Ernie Tomasso packed up his instruments and left them for Fred to load onto the coach. The next morning Ernie came to me and told me, "Fred's gone without paying the landlady." I said, "Don't worry, I'll pay it and deduct it from his wages." Little did I know, until later, that he had absconded and taken Ernie's clarinet and alto sax with him. Obviously the theft had to be reported and, sad to say, Fred was arrested just a couple of hours later with the instruments still in his possession. I've never been able to understand why he did it. He had a good job which he sacrificed in a moment of thinking he could get away with his theft. Manifestly, he was suffering some psychological disorder.

After that a young Australian joined us as road manager. He did a good job while he lasted – he was working his way around the world. Once, on a long journey up north, it had been snowing incessantly. Taffy was having a difficult time of it driving when suddenly from the back came an Australian voice shouting, "Stop the coach!" We all thought that something serious had happened and Taffy brought the vehicle to a skidding halt. Out shot our roadie, pulling open the coach door. He rolled himself over and over in a snowdrift and then walked back saying, "The folks back home would love this!" Of course, he'd never seen snow.

Accidents are always a safe bet for attracting publicity. One in which we were involved occurred after a gig in Hereford. It involved a singer, Ann Haven, who had been a member of the Pieces of Eight but had just joined Geraldo. She appeared with us impromptu in a concert at Hereford on the Sunday night, no doubt completely contrary to the terms of her contract with Geraldo. The following day she was scheduled to broadcast with his band. A friend from Monaco had brought her to Hereford.

After the concert, she and her friend offered to give Laurie and me a lift back to London. It was quite a journey. As we approached a roundabout en route for Uxbridge it started to rain. The driver, who I'll call Pierre, was travelling very fast and obviously didn't see the 'slow down' sign. He braked sharply and we went into a tremendous skid and mounted the roundabout. The passenger door opened with the impact and I shot out, followed by Ann. I landed on my shoulder and lost a shoe. On getting up, I could see that Ann was pinned under the front wheels, so I went into the road to try to get help from a passing vehicle. Pierre was OK but Laurie, who was on the back seat, was unconscious with a nasty gash over his good eye. I thought, "My God, I hope he's going to be all right. If he loses that eye, he'll be blind." At that moment an ambulance arrived, no doubt called by another motorist.

We had to concoct a story to protect Ann from Geraldo's wrath. One garbled version of it in the press was that she was returning to London from visiting her parents in Scotland and Laurie and I had joined her on the journey for a lift to town. Another was that she had been paying us a visit in 'Hertford'. But it's hard to see how we could travel from Hertford, north of London, and crash on Western Avenue, which is west of London.

Before the accident the journey was eventful enough. We were trying to find the main road through a small town but the road signs were well hidden behind trees. Eventually I said to Pierre, "You're going the wrong way. This is a one way street. But we're nearly at the end of it and nobody is about, so you might as well carry on." As luck would have it, a policeman with outstretched arms was standing at the end of the street, inviting us to stop. Pierre said, "Nobody speak." The cop came over, looked into the open window on the driver's side and said, "Do you know you've come up a one way street?" In reply, Pierre let out a stream of what, I assume, was his native French dialect. The officer of the law looked nonplussed. "Does anyone here speak English?" he asked. After a pregnant silence and feeling that something should be done I said, "I spick a leetle." He looked me straight in the eye. "Tell your friend here that he has come up a one way street." This forced me to gabble a lot of meaningless sounds (I have only a modicum of French), making with the shrugging shoulders. Pierre nodded his understanding. "Carry on," said the policemen. "I won't book you this time but be more careful in future." With that kind gesture he sent us on to our date with destiny.

Changing Faces

Over the years I had to cope with the need to replace musicians whom I loved working with in the Pieces of Eight but who had to leave. Geoff Love's departure had been a major blow. Another came when Norrie Paramor told me, some time around 1950, that he would have to leave. In a way, I knew it was inevitable. I myself often felt I wanted to settle down to a more permanent home life. But Geoff and Norrie had been partners. Their replacements could only be employees and so a different relationship existed. Norrie promised he would stay until a suitable replacement could be found. He also said he would help me in any way possible afterwards, and he kept his promise. We tried out several pianists at audition but without success. At this time, Ted Darrah, who hailed from Belfast, was our trombonist. Ted said, "I know a pianist who would suit you. He's from my home town and he's very good. His name is Jimmy McKnight."

On that recommendation, Jimmy was contacted. I asked him to play a try-out gig with us in the west country. He arrived well before the dance started and we decided to audition him immediately. While we were playing, who should walk in but Leslie 'Jiver' Hutchinson, with trumpet and suitcase in hand.[3] I asked, "What are you doing here?" thinking that he must have come in to hear our band while he was playing somewhere in the area.

It wasn't the case. He said, "I'm playing here tonight with my band." Well, I had already seen my contract and the publicity outside the hall, so I said, "I didn't know there were

---

[3] West Indian trumpeter and vocalist Leslie 'Jiver' Hutchinson was working mainly with Geraldo during the early 1950s. He also worked at this time with Geoff Love and led his own group. He was active with his own bands through the 1950s until he died in a band bus accident in Norwich in 1959 (Ed.)

two bands booked. Are you sure?" He took out his diary and had a look. "Oh no," he groaned. "It's next week and I've booked my hotel room. I'll have to stay. There are no trains back to London tonight, anyway." The upshot was that he sat in with our band and had a ball. He also commented on Jimmy McKnight's playing. He said, "He's good. Where did you get him?" We had already made up our collective minds so Jimmy was in.

Mainly drummers came and went more frequently than other musicians. I've always considered the drummer the most important member of a rhythm section. He has to be the anchor. Some drummers didn't measure up to that requirement and had to go within a short time. But those who did were always in demand, particularly for residential jobs and recording. You could count them on the fingers of one hand. Danny Craig, Johnny Wise, Tony Lytton and Joe Gibbons were in that category.

Eventually Ernie and Freddie Tomasso left too. But I have to tell a story or two about Ernie before moving on. He had unusual ideas about protecting himself from the rigours of touring. He experimented with exercises and diets. For a while he was a vegetarian. Then he just ate fruit. The contents of what we called his nosebag kept getting modified. The guessing game became a gambling one, with odds on what would be his next change on the healthy living front. Suddenly he changed course. He bought a high powered motor bike and ceased travelling with the rest of us. So he had to get a helmet, black waterproof trousers, over jacket and boots. I pleaded with him that he should allow enough time to arrive at venues to start playing at the appointed time. He not only had to take off all his (sometimes wet and muddy) clobber but also clean up to put on his band uniform.

One of our gigs was at a posh hotel in Harrogate. It was a cinch for Ernie and Freddie as it was very close to their home town, Leeds. Freddie arrived dressed and ready for work, having come by train. Not so Ernie. Laurie, Norrie Paramor, Geoff Love and I were sitting in the dining room of the hotel waiting for an ordered meal to be delivered. The hotel decor was very expensive. In particular there was a beautiful white carpet. Suddenly something looking like a visitor from outer space appeared in the restaurant entrance. At least for us, it seemed as though the world had stopped. It was Ernie. He made straight for us, striding across that beautiful carpet in his riding trappings and wet boots. He reached our table just as the waiter was putting out the dishes. He said, "Where's the 'all and what time are we on?"

With some embarrassment I got up, signalled to him to follow me out of the restaurant and walked along the corridor to the entrance to the hall, which was clearly indicated. With more than a little anger I told him the starting time and went back to my meal. All members of the band had a weekly schedule with times of starting, names of towns and venues and other important information. So there was no need for that pantomime entrance. For years, musicians used to say, "All bandleaders are bastards." But sometimes bandleaders have a tough time too.

On the road, we visited most towns in Britain, Scotland and Ireland. In the case of Ireland, we crossed the sea two or three times a year. It was with pleasant anticipation and for some it was a returning home.

On one visit in 1954 we played the City Hall Derry. The other band there was led by Ulster's fine clarinettist Gay McIntyre. In a way, it was a family band. The members were brothers or cousins and all of them were great players. I was listening to them prior to taking over for our stint, when I heard the young trumpeter Joe McIntyre play a solo that showed great depth of feeling and a gorgeous full tone. Laurie, standing beside me, was equally impressed. I said, "Laurie, I'd love to have him in our band. I'd like to talk to him. Try and get him over for a chat during the change over.

Young Joe was sixteen years of age, with very boyish features and complexion. I thought he would be a tremendous asset. He came to talk and we shook hands. I asked him how he would like to join our band. He looked at me with astonishment. He obviously couldn't believe what he was hearing and said, "I would love to, but I don't think I'm good enough." I told him I wanted him to join us but first I must talk to Gay and to his father.

In the meantime I talked to Bruts Gonella, who was our trumpeter at the time,[4] and told him what was in my mind. I suggested that maybe we could make a swap: Bruts to join Gay's band and Joe to join me. The Gay McIntyres was a very good band and had a lot of work all over the country. Of course, it would depend on Gay's attitude. It worked. Gay was happy and so was Bruts and it now depended on Joe McIntyre senior. When we met, he said that he thought Joe was too young to leave the country but he would let him go if I undertook to look after him. I promised I would. He would live with us. The deal was settled with handshakes all round and no-one hurt.

Joe stayed in our flat for a while while I took time out to coach him on his reading. But Laurie thought it might be better if Joe stayed in his house as there was more room there. So the change was made. My son David was a frequent visitor at Laurie's house and Joe and he became close pals.

---

[4] Like his more famous brother, Nat, Bruts Gonella had a very extensive and successful career as a trumpeter from the beginning of the 1930s until the 1980s. He played with the Pieces of Eight from November 1952 until the spring of 1954. He joined Sid Willmot's band in Manchester in May 1954 and settled there, later moving to Brighton. In 1964 he emigrated to Australia (Ed.).

As I had anticipated, Joe was a great success with audiences everywhere and always got a big hand for his solos, whether melodic or jazz. He was a lovely young man who never thought himself as good as he really was. He didn't get above himself at any time and always kept his cool. Strangely enough, I found that to be characteristic in most people I worked with on either side of the border in Ireland.

My first tour of Eire was arranged by a student at Trinity College Dublin, named Sean Hoban. He needed to make some money to help him through university and asked what I would charge for playing a gig in the Mansion House. I didn't want to discourage him and quoted the lowest fee I could. But, as I didn't know him, I told him I needed to be paid 'up front'. He agreed and with the help of fellow students and a college band the gig was a tremendous success financially. That really got him going. He asked me to quote for a tour beginning and ending in Dublin. Again I said I'd need some money in advance and he agreed. I think some money was put up by his college friends. I felt sorry for Sean. His father was the Mayor of Westport, Co. Mayo, and owned several shops and the only cinema there. He wanted Sean to stay at home and help run the businesses. In a way, it was a replica of my own early life.

We went ahead with the tour and the night before returning to Dublin we travelled to Westport to play in the cinema despite Mayor Hoban's misgivings. On arriving, long before the doors were due to be opened, we saw a long queue extending from the cinema entrance all the way down the hill. The evening was a sell-out and a triumph for the 'wayward' youth. That night, the Mayor relented. We were all invited to his house for a celebratory party and he promised to help Sean. Now Sean Hoban is a well known doctor in Dublin with another surgery in America. We are good friends, communicating and visiting frequently. As ye sow, so shall ye reap.

While on that tour, we played a one night stand in the Crystal Ballroom in Dublin's South Ann Street. There I first heard Jon Clarke sing. He was a personality with a good voice and I was determined to recruit him. He joined the Pieces of Eight a couple of weeks later.

Non-Stop

So it was seemingly endless travelling. The lure of the road is like a large magnet dragging a tiny piece of metal: the Regal Cinema Minehead, the Winter Gardens Penzance, the Orchid Ballroom Purley, the King Edward Horse Hotel Windsor, the Savoy Ballroom Southsea, Hornsey Town Hall London – a typical week's work. You name them; we played them! And we entertained. I have a newspaper cutting about a July 1953 return visit by the Pieces to Penzance. It is headed 'TRIUMPH OF PIECES OF EIGHT' and goes on:

> Well, they did it! Play the Gay Gordons that is. Pompitty, Pompitty, Pompitty just like the 1930s. But a few other eras were represented too; the days when Chicago was the home of modern jazz and 1953 when 'The Champ' meant the same thing. It was all great fun.

It was tiring and sometimes so to the point of exhaustion but, because each venue was different with different audiences, it was enjoyable. I'm not sure that the rest of the band always felt the same. After all, it was my band and thinking about it now a lot of the attraction was due to the adulation of the crowds and the almost fawning requests for autographs and photos. It wasn't always fun when we had to travel in bad weather. We continually checked the newspapers for information on weather conditions, but also of course for mentions of our performances or any pictures published; a kind of self-adulation, if you like.

We were also involved in accidents that got into the newspapers. I mentioned earlier the Ann Haven episode in which Laurie and I were involved. There was also a nasty crash at the end of August 1953, involving Danny Craig and some of the chaps from the band. Danny was driving them in his car from Warrington to Glasgow for our two week engagement at Green's Playhouse. The headline ran, "FIVE GOLD MUSICIANS NARROW ESCAPE IN CAR CRASH'. The report said that Danny's Chevrolet had wrapped itself around a telegraph pole. It was badly damaged but fortunately no-one was seriously injured. There were just minor cuts and varying degrees of shock. The damage amounted to about £300 which, by today's prices would be more than £3,000. The report went on to say:

> Then came the Good Samaritan. A brilliantly inspired tipster told Danny and Laurie Gold so convincingly that Darius would win the Two Thousand Guineas that Danny rushed to get his thirty pounds out of the bank. Even the careful Laurie sported a fiver. Darius won at eight to one. Let's see. £30 times 8 = £240, so Happy Motoring Days are here again for Danny.

Despite the accident we all reached Glasgow in good time to instal our instruments, go to our respective digs, clean up and eat. The road manager and Taffy the driver had set up the stand ready for us to perform. I went to the pub close to Green's for a dose of dutch courage. It was my first appearance in the Playhouse with my own band so I felt nervous. I also knew about the protection racket which had operated there with other bandleaders and I wondered when I would be approached. While I was at the bar ordering my drink I noticed that another man next to me had an empty glass. With an impulsive gesture I invited him to have a drink and he accepted. During the conversation that ensued he asked what I was doing in Glasgow. I said, "I'm the bandleader at Green's. I'm starting this afternoon." He said, "You didn't know me and yet you offered me a drink. I'll tell you right now, you'll not be bothered while you're in Glasgow." It transpired that he was the top man in the local protection business. At night, after the show, I walked to my digs along Sauchiehall Street, followed by two 'heavies' who had been assigned to see me back safely. How lucky can you get?

For our performances at the Playhouse we were required to augment to bring the size of the band to fourteen pieces. That required considerable preparation. It meant writing band parts for the additional personnel, as well as booking musicians. We hired players from the Glasgow pool to avoid the additional costs of fares had we brought musicians from London.

The engagement was very well advertised daily in the local newspapers and brought in the crowds. It ended to great acclaim and with the hint that there would certainly be a return visit. In the meantime it was back to the road. After Maxine Russell left she was replaced as our singer by Margaret Rose, who had been recommended by the bandleader Ivy Benson. Margaret joined us on a trial basis for a gig at an American camp at Burtonwood, proved satisfactory and became a permanent member.

By the mid-1950s I was finding the one nighters ever more gruelling. I began to think seriously about giving it all up. I thought, "If I do, it will be the end of the Pieces of Eight." I knew it would be a fateful decision but I would have to be resolute if I took the plunge. Meanwhile the pattern remained as before: dances on weekdays, concerts on Sundays and the occasional broadcast or recording. I was longing to get back to Theobalds Road. The children were growing up and I was needed at home more than ever.

The end came on a late gig one night in 1955. I was feeling very tired and under a lot of pressure and I told Laurie I wanted to give the band up. I asked him, "How would you like to take it over?" He looked startled for a moment, thought a bit longer and finally said he would give it a try. We agreed that my last appearance with the band would be on New Year's Eve. Laurie would take over from the beginning of 1956. But for the moment we kept this plan to ourselves.

Mentioning Laurie here reminds me of a story going the rounds about one of the lumbers he perpetrated on the unwary. As I explained earlier, he lost an eye from a childhood accident. So he wears an artificial one and keeps a spare in a box. We were having a pub lunch one day with Lennie Felix, our pianist at the time. When Lennie had his back turned, Laurie slipped the spare eye into Lennie's glass of beer. Lennie gradually drained his glass and, as he did so, the eye appeared, staring up through the beer. He dropped the glass in shock.[5] Everyone in the bar saw the funny side except Lennie but he got his revenge while we were on our way to a gig in the north of England. Laurie was reading a detective story and getting towards the really exciting part where the great denouement would take place. As he reached the climax of the story he found that all the rest of the pages were missing and went apoplectic with the frustration. Lennie eventually owned up, all was forgiven in good humour, and the missing pages were handed back.

In the final years before I handed over to Laurie we trekked the country, sometimes in the most bizarre conditions. On one occasion we were returning to London from Eastbourne to perform at a concert the following day at the Gaumont Lewisham. It was a Saturday night and there was a thick fog. A newspaper report, headed "A THICK, THICK FOG IN LONDON" described our exploits:

[5] Laurie's glass eye may have stared up through a good many musicians' drinks in its time. Saxophonist Billy Amstell (in his *Don't Fuss Mr. Ambrose*) tells of the eye appearing at the bottom of his cup of tea at a break in a recording session at the Aeolian Hall (Ed.).

The Harry Gold Band found getting to Eastbourne easy enough on Saturday, and getting back wasn't so bad until they reached Croydon, where the fog clamped down and visibility was nil. Reluctant to agree to the driver's suggestion that they should wait till morning, the boys organised themselves to walk in front of the coach two at a time, with towels draped round them for the driver to see and follow. That way, they got from Croydon (3.00 a.m.) into town (7.00 a.m.) in four hours.

Then there was another frantic rush to get to the Gaumont, Lewisham for the Sunday concert. The paper wrote:

They got there alright − by train − but the lorry carrying uniforms and instruments fell by the wayside and got lost in the fog around Lambeth Way. Frantic phone calls resulted in the gear being transferred to a train at Waterloo. The minutes ticked by with no news of the train's arrival. Harry made tentative arrangements with the Nat Gonella Band, also on the bill, to borrow some of their instruments, when, twenty minutes before they were due on stage, they learned that at last the train − and their equipment − had arrived at Lewisham. Out they dashed to the station, grabbed uniforms and instruments, raced back to the theatre, and appeared on stage exactly on schedule with none of the audience any the wiser.

Even when we were relaxing, life was not necessarily ordinary. I remember a notable incident involving our trombonist of the time, Pete Hodge.[6] One night, after the band's performance, he decided to go fishing. He must have looked a strange sight because he was wearing the tartan jacket band uniform while sitting, completely relaxed, fishing at dead of night in some remote spot. Anyway, a policeman saw him and tapped him on the shoulder. It was the middle of December and well after midnight, and he was subjected to a cross-examination. The policeman thought Pete had escaped from a mental institution. The strange thing is that he and that

[6] Pete Hodge worked with the Pieces of Eight, under Harry's leadership, from 1953 to 1955, and under Laurie Gold, during 1956 (Ed.).

same policeman met again after 32 years, in a pub while Pete was on holiday. Small world.

And Finally...

Certainly there were some quieter times breaking up the life on the road. We had two more stays at Green's Playhouse in Glasgow. And there was the lovely relaxation of a two week residency in the Rialto Dance Hall in Belfast, followed by two weeks at the Fiesta, also in Belfast. So that was a whole month of peace and quiet and, of course, the normal busy playing schedule had its compensations in some memorable occasions. One was when we worked with the American pianist Teddy Wilson, who visited Britain for a 17 day tour. Four bands were chosen to accompany him for the London debut: Freddy Randall, Basil Kirchin (then leading his band at Fountainbridge Palais, Edinburgh), trumpeter Kenny Baker with his then New Quartet, and the Pieces of Eight.[7] The *Melody Maker* commented:

> Making their first concert appearance at the Royal Albert Hall will be Harry Gold and His Pieces of Eight, to accompany Teddy Wilson in his British debut on Sunday September 20. Incidentally, on the same night as the Royal Albert Hall concert, Teddy Wilson will also be appearing at the Savoy Cinema, Burnt Oak, Edgware, supported by Harry Gold and His Pieces of Eight.

I'm still trying to work that one out, unless the first concert was in the afternoon.

---

[7] The concert was held on September 20th 1953. Permission for it was obtained, despite a ban, in force since 1934, on foreign jazz and dance band musicians working in Britain, because Wilson was considered a 'variety' artist. Reports at the time indicated that 7,000 people attended the concert. See Godbolt, *History* II, p. 183 (Ed.).

One of our tours was a week in Ireland in February 1953, booked by Bill Fuller who owned the Crystal Ballroom in Dublin, among several others. We went over by the night boat which arrived at Dun Laoghaire at about six o'clock in the morning. We knew that we would be met at the port to be taken to the first gig at Red Island, a short ride by car. With plenty of time to relax before the boat docked, we decided to have breakfast on board before disembarking. Sure enough, on leaving the gang plank we were overwhelmed with welcoming handshakes and led to three cars. There was also a small truck for the instruments and personal baggage, which were loaded by the welcoming committee. We were driven to digs where we would stay for the night. The landlady, hands folded and with a beaming smile, was waiting at the door. "Good morning, gentlemen," she said. "Your breakfast is ready. You must be hungry with the travelling all night." So we sat down to a second breakfast – a full Irish one of bacon, sausage, black pudding, white pudding, eggs, etc. – with foreboding. She stood watching us, beaming, making sure we finished the lot. With heavy hearts and stomachs we did, and then decided to go for a walk to help digestion.

It was Sunday morning and there wasn't a soul about. We thought most of the population would be in church, so we wandered along the deserted main street, parallel with the sea front. At one street corner there was a clear view of the sea and, nearby, a pub. While we debated whether to walk to the sea shore a face appeared in the pub window, indicating to us to turn towards a row of green painted wooden doors, a little further along the street. It was clear that we were being invited. "Which door do we want?" we asked ourselves but a passerby pointed to a hole in one of the doors and said, conspiratorily, "Put your finger through that hole and lift the latch." Opening the door, we found ourselves in the back of the pub. It was packed with drinkers and someone was playing an accordion. The joint was jumping at ten o'clock on Sunday morning. No doubt the church opposite the pub was also full. We were directed to a table and serious drinking of pints of delicious Guinness began. At twelve o'clock, the landlord opened the pub's front door, came over and declared, "You're OK, fellas. You're now drinking legally." That could only happen in Ireland, I think.

The tour ended on the Saturday night in the now-demolished Arcadia in Cork. It was a huge ballroom which boasted two bandstands on separate balconies, high above the dance floor. The layout was designed to leave as much room as possible for the dancers. That night, I was told by the management that they had had to close the doors when the maximum number of 1,000 people were in the hall. It was wonderful to look down on the dancing couples moving to the beat of the jazz. I think that, like the Scots, Irish people have a natural feeling for dancing, probably because of the traditions of their native music. Louis Armstrong once paid a great tribute to that innate feeling. He said, when asked about it, that Scottish music is heavily rhythmic and it follows that its players have to be also. I think that applies no less to Irish music and its performers, as evidenced recently by the enormous success of the Riverdance company.

The Cork gig ended at 2.30 a.m. on Sunday morning and there was a frantic rush to pack instruments, music stands and other necessaries for a charity show that same night in Liverpool in aid of cancer research. The *Melody Maker* had sent their reporter and cameraman Chris Hayes with us on the Irish tour and he covered our Liverpool gig too. His story, headlined "OPERATION GOLD-LIFT", in *MM* read: "How to get from Cork to Liverpool in a matter of hours? That was the problem facing Harry Gold... last Sunday. The answer was obvious – for the air is the road for the one night stand of 1953."

We loaded our instruments on to the luggage trailer in pouring rain at half past three in the morning, made the seven hour drive to Dublin, and flew to Liverpool, where we played two sessions for an audience of 3,000 at the charity concert. A photo in *Melody Maker* showed poor Chris Hayes, exhausted, surrounded by our altoist Alan Doniger, Ernie Tomasso, Danny Craig and me, and declaring that his next assignment would be to take photos for a beauty parade, because, "you get more sleep" than travelling with Harry Gold's Pieces of Eight.

On New Year's Eve 1955, this frantic life of travelling and touring came to an end for me. It was the parting of the ways and we all felt the sadness. It showed in the playing. Every member of the band had empathetically reacted to my innermost thoughts with the result that the band had lost its sparkle. I felt I needed to go off stage for a large drop of the amber liquid that revives so I said to Laurie, "Would you take over for a while? I'll be back soon." My leaving the stand had an effect on the band. I could tell that they needed to adjust and get back to their normal way of playing, but without me. When I left the bandstand it made them realise that was how it would be from then on. They rallied to Laurie and that made me feel a lot better. During our interval break, I got them all to the bar and bought a round. Of course the first round was followed by a couple more. By that time we were all in good spirits (no pun intended). I made a farewell speech and wished them the best of luck for the future. It was then that I discovered they had subscribed to give me a going away present – a lovely table lamp suitable for use while writing music.

8.

STAYING PUT – SOME OF THE TIME

So I went home – to stay. It is hard to convey on paper the excitement from the children and the pleasure Peggy felt in the realisation that I was going to stay put. It also worked that way for me. It took a few days to settle down to home life routine and a regular job of taking the boys to school in the morning. I also realised that I had to find work so I started visiting Archer Street and let it be known that I was available. I phoned publishers and the BBC's arranging department and soon some work was coming my way. Then – a bit of luck – I had a call from a music publisher, David Toff, who asked if I would like a resident job in his office in Newman Street, off Oxford Street. Corn in Egypt! It meant regular wages and doing the occasional gig.

In David Toff's office I was introduced to Bobby Murphy, a musician I had known in Dublin who was now living in London. For a second, Bobby and I stared at each other in disbelief and then there were shouts of "It's you. Jaysus, I don't believe it!" and much hugging and laughter. Dave asked, "Do you know one another?", which immediately produced more howls of hysterical laughter. When we had quietened down and Bobby had found out that I was going to be his side-kick, he whispered, "It'll be lunch time at one o'clock. We'll go over to Mooneys and reminisce over a jar or two and a sandwich." No work was done until after lunch. I had to organise my seating arrangements and learn the office routine. It seemed that both of us had to do copying as well as writing scores, because Dave did not employ a permanent copyist. So we would be kept busy.

Neither of us could wait patiently for one o'clock. We were like a couple of kids going off for our holidays and we left the office early to drink Guinness and eat sandwiches while catching up on each other's news. Joint visits to Mooneys became routine until one day Dave said, "This can't continue. One of you must be here at all times." That ended the lunch time sprees except on St. Patrick's Day and Christmas Eve.

At that time Bobby was also leading a band at the Blarney Club in Tottenham Court Road. When his tenor player decided to leave, he asked me if I'd like to join the band on tenor and clarinet. He said that the money wasn't great but the job was enjoyable. Apart from music for normal ballroom dancing, we had to play Irish music for reels, jigs, barn dances and a kind of round dance called the 'Siege of Ennis' which required a 'caller'.

Nine to Five

Now I had two jobs. The one in the office started at 9.00 a.m. and finished at 5.00 p.m. That meant I could get home for an evening meal and change for the Blarney Club because our flat was only a short bus ride from the office and the club. I decided to buy a bicycle which could be chained on railings, but using it became a problem sometimes as far as the Blarney was concerned because the musicians customarily spent the half hour break in the nearby pub. There were times when I could be seen walking my bike home along New Oxford Street because I wasn't up to riding it safely. Still, as Bobby had predicted, it was fun.

Having become an arranger in a publisher's office soon brought other rewards. I had begun to become known as a general arranger in every kind of style. Consequently, broadcasting bandleaders would sometimes phone asking for a special arrangement of a currently popular song. The payment would be met by the publisher who would benefit by at least three broadcasts of that tune. It was a kind of 'plugging' and, for me, it was lucrative. So I was working harder than ever, but at least I wasn't rushing around the country.

In the meantime, Bobby Murphy had returned to Dublin to work for Radio Telefis Eirann, conducting their Light Music Orchestra. I found that, after his departure, the office work was too much to handle. I had to ask David Toff to engage an additional arranger or at least a copyist. I suggested Bill Kirkpatrick, a saxophonist who was also a composer and who would be willing to come in as a copyist. Bill later became a top ranking osteopath, but his career in that regard hadn't yet begun and Dave Toff took him on.

One morning, Bill came to the office with the news that he was organising a saxophone quartet to perform classical music in schools. He asked me if I would like to be involved and I agreed since it was a new direction for me and it looked interesting. It didn't take long to get a programme into shape and very soon we got the first string of dates. It turned out well because, to our surprise, the students were enthusiastic. I suppose it was the interest of the saxophones and I must say that Bill had an excellent way of handling the youngsters. He encouraged them to ask questions and even handle his saxophone. I wouldn't have had the courage.

The first series of concerts in London schools began in the spring of 1957. A typical programme might include selections from Chopin, Schubert, Schumann and Brahms and items such as Pierné's 'Parade of the Little Lead Soldiers', Ibert's 'The Little White Donkey', and so on. Ralph Bruce, the clarinettist from the early years of the Pieces of Eight, was our altoist. Bill played soprano sax, Jay Langham handled the baritone, and I was the tenorist. We got plenty of favourable publicity and the quartet was booked again for another series of concerts in the autumn.

So for a time my life was one of boring regularity: occasional concerts with the saxophone quartet, nine-to-five work in David Toff's office, and then eight until midnight at the Blarney Club. There wasn't even a fight to relieve the monotony. But I couldn't complain. The money was good and I was at home with the family.

I knew it was too good to last. Suddenly fate decided to take a hand. Firstly, the school concerts ended because of a new policy from County Hall, where London local government was based. Then I was told by Mr. Toff that he would have to make a staff cut and that I was to be the victim. Finally, the Blarney Club closed its doors and I had nothing.

When I was in the Oxford Street area, I continued to visit my old friend Ivor Mairants in his guitar shop, Ivor Mairants' Musicentre, in Rathbone Place. One day he said to me, "Harry, I can't bear to see you doing nothing. How would you like to come into business?" I have to say that I've never been a businessman and I couldn't see how I would fit in, but the offer was tempting. It was like a drowning man being thrown a rope, so I said I would give it a try.

At Ivor's suggestion, I took home a huge quantity of guitar literature – price lists, styles, and so on – and studied it all so that I could be familiar with the complete range of guitars he sold and their prices. He also had an immense library of printed guitar music, from classical to jazz, the catalogue of which which I was required to memorise. I spent a weekend going through the material, and the following Monday arrived at the door for the 9.00 a.m. opening only to find two of the staff waiting outside and the door not open. It was pouring with rain and we chatted for a while wondering how we could get shelter. I was told this was a regular occurrence. Ivor never opened the shop himself. His son Stuart was the manager and was supposed to open up but was never on time. I resolved to have a quiet word with Mr. Mairants. Although I needed a job, I wasn't prepared to stand outside in every kind of climatic condition.

Ivor asked me if I would be prepared to hold the keys to the shop and open up each day. I foolishly said yes. I discovered that my name had to be registered with the police as a key holder. They needed my address and phone number in case of emergency, which was unfortunate because I lived so close and could be called at any time after closing.

There was an incident which put me in real trouble. I arrived as usual one Monday morning and opened the door after going through the burglar alarm routine, only to find some open guitar cases on the floor and one case empty. I checked the label and saw that it was a very expensive classical guitar that was missing. I thought that Ivor might have called in to take it, as he occasionally did, to use for a recording session but I phoned him just to be certain. He said he hadn't taken it and I told him he had better come at once. I couldn't understand why the alarm had not worked. Neither could the police and I was in the hot seat.

Two detectives came to the shop to question me. I knew they would as, apart from Ivor, I was the only registered key holder. It was very fortunate for me that on the day of the break-in I was playing on a gig booked by the dockers' union on a boat sailing to Calais and there were about 3,000 people on board to vouch for that. Nevertheless, until proof could be forthcoming, I was suspect number one.

It is nerve-wracking being put through the meat-grinder knowing full well that you are innocent and yet being made to feel guilty. The police came three times with questions to catch me out. They asked who else knew where the keys were and who lived with me. I explained that my two boys lived with my wife and me, that they were also on the Calais boat at the time and that there were witnesses to the fact. Nevertheless the police went to my sons' places of employment to check on them. Until the last visit we were all suspects. Then it was discovered that there was a caretaker for the whole building and when the police visited him they found stolen property from other office occupants, and a guitar. They didn't apologise to me for their aggression. I had a feeling that Ivor thought I might have had a hand in the theft, because from my point of view the atmosphere between him and me now seemed cool. I decided I would leave at the earliest opportunity, which came soon afterwards.

Arranging at EMI

My son David worked as a music copyist at EMI. He told me there was a vacancy for an arranger so I went after it. I knew the pianist and arranger Gordon Rees who was manager of the relevant department. We discussed salary, which was considerably more than I was getting at Ivor's shop, so I started with EMI the following week. I was very pleased to be away because, apart from anything else, I was really out of my depth in the guitar business. The new job was interesting and enjoyable, the guys in the office were friendly and Gordon started me immediately on orchestrating for large orchestras with string sections. I also began to get private work in a field similar to that with which I had been involved in the Paramor-Gold office. At the same time, publishers started to offer arranging commissions of special dixieland scores for print. So here I was working hard again but living at home. And I was once again a musician – not a salesman, as I had been in the guitar shop.

While I worked at EMI I still led bands occasionally for particular events. I put together a group I called the New Beat Band to take advantage of the craze for jiving and I played soprano sax to give that group a different sound. But I thought I had finished with the Pieces of Eight when I handed them over to Laurie. I was wrong about that. Occasionally, when there was no possibility of any clash with what Laurie was doing with his band, I used the Pieces of Eight name for my gigs. I did that when I played summer seasons at Scarborough in 1958 and 1959, because Laurie wouldn't be affected by a band playing for a limited period and in that town only.

Then, out of the blue, the BBC offered me a live television broadcast on their pop music show, 'The Six-Five Special' from a dance hall in Glasgow. As it was a TV show and good publicity I decided to take it provided I could get some other work in Glasgow to pay for the cost of transport etc. I knew that the BBC money would not be good enough for a one-off show.

At the time of the TV show, Laurie was working with his band in a residency at the Locarno Ballroom, Sheffield. So I decided to take the risk of calling the group I used for the television broadcast Harry Gold and His Pieces of Eight. It was probably tempting confusion. During the television broadcast the BBC commere Josephine Douglas introduced me and my band as *Laurie* Gold and His Pieces of Eight. This caused consternation everywhere. The next day, the Sheffield *Daily Herald*'s reporter wrote, under the headline "GOLD RUSH WASN'T WHAT IT SEEMED":

> Just Jo's little slip. Whew! I heard how the Six-Five Special did the 200-mile trip from Glasgow to Sheffield in ten minutes. At 6.50, Laurie Gold's band was still playing for hundreds of teenage rock 'n' rollers in the BBC Television Six-Five Show in Glasgow. At 7, they took the stand at a Sheffield ballroom in their immaculate tartan jackets, looking quite unruffled. There was not a sign of travel fatigue. Seven hundred dancers were amazed.

But, as Laurie explained to me, the trouble was Harry − his brother Harry. "The BBC dropped a clanger alright," he said. "Commere Josephine Douglas introduced Harry to nine million viewers as me, Laurie. I'm sorry for Harry but I can see how the mistake happened."

It shows that the television presenters hadn't done their homework and as a result I lost an opportunity. Still, you can't win 'em all. I suppose I felt that the Pieces of Eight name was too good not to use if the right opportunity arose. Certainly it was memorable and people had some fun with it. One comedy radio show used to mention our band name regularly, coming up with ever more bizarre variations week by week. We became Harry Coal and His Pieces of Slate, Harry Bald and His Pieces of Pate, Harry Cod and His Pieces of Skate, etc., etc.

One radio broadcast with the band, in early 1960, not only produced better publicity than the 'Six-Five Special' fiasco but had some interesting consequences. During the show Betty Taylor sang my arrangement of 'Basin Street Blues' and, out of the blue, a letter of thanks came from the song's composer, Spencer Williams. He was then living in Sweden. He had heard the programme and was enthusiastic about the band. Of course, I replied. What followed was a suggestion from Spencer that we should collaborate in songwriting. He said he had lost his sight and needed a writing partner. I let him know I was interested and he visited me en route for New York. We developed a close friendship from that time and, between us, wrote half a dozen songs. None of them saw the light of day − the publishers weren't at all interested − but we stayed friends until he passed away in 1965.

While I was still at EMI, I renewed contact with Bobby Murphy, my old Dublin mate, who phoned one day to ask if I could help with some orchestrations. As conductor for the light orchestra of Radio Telefis Eirann he needed a large repertoire for the many programmes with which he was involved. Having worked in a music publisher's office he knew that there would be a large library of music on file in my office at EMI. He asked me to look out for things he could use. So I sent photocopies of new material. It was an arrangement of mutual advantage for him and for EMI. He could vary his programmes at no cost to himself and EMI would gain from the royalties from the performances.

Some time later, Bobby called again, this time in a panic. He said, "Do you think you could get over here immediately?" I asked why, thinking that this was a lot to ask given my job commitments. He explained that a new Irish musical called 'Carrie' was due to be staged at the Gaiety Theatre in Dublin and that they had been let down with the commissioned orchestrations which had turned out to be completely unsuitable. Bobby said, "The opening night is only ten days away and in the meantime the cast is having to rehearse with only piano accompaniment." He had told the producer that I was the only orchestrator he knew who could work quickly. Now he was phoning to ask me to help.

The upshot was that I asked Gordon Rees for permission to take my two weeks holiday in these circumstances and he agreed. Then I had to arrange the contract conditions which I needed to have in writing. I needed somewhere to stay, payment of the air fare and access to a piano and I quoted a fee much higher than I would normally have asked because of the rush which was not conducive to the relaxed conditions that writing needed. To my surprise the producer agreed to everything I asked.

The composer of the songs for the musical thought that it would be best if I stayed in his house in case of problems that might arise with the music. So I was given a very comfortable bedroom and the exclusive use of his lounge which contained a lovely grand piano. His two young children were forbidden to come anywhere near the lounge while I was working there. I woke at 6.00 a.m. every morning and after a cup of tea and a shower I slogged away all day, stopping only for more cups of tea and quick snacks until eleven at night.

An army of music copyists was engaged to stand by as pages of score were available from me, for them to extract the individual instrumental parts. As soon as a full set of parts was finished, it was delivered to the theatre for rehearsal. It was like a factory, with me as the machine. Finally, on the tenth day, I finished the *pièce de résistance*, the overture which had necessitated some original composition on my part.

The dress rehearsal was due to start that evening. I was asked to attend in case there were any errors needing correction. Eventually the overture parts arrived, with some nervous anticipation all round. The pages were distributed to the musicians who were all excellent players and up went the conductor's baton to start the rehearsal performance. To my complete surprise there was only one copyist's mistake which was easily rectified and, with a sigh of relief, we all repaired to the nearest pub after the rehearsal was completed.

I was given a box in the theatre for the first performance and, togged out in a borrowed dinner suit, I anxiously waited for the opening bars. You know, there is nothing more satisfying than to hear your music being well played and the applause from the audience. At the end of the show there were the usual calls for the author followed by the speeches. Then I was introduced to the audience with the words: "Ladies and gentlemen, I have to tell you that in the box up there is a little man named Harry Gold who has worked hard for the past ten days on the music you heard tonight. If it hadn't been for his efforts, tonight's show wouldn't have been possible." I had to stand up to my full five foot two, my head only just above the edge of the box, to acknowledge a tumultuous cheering and hand clapping. It was worth every minute of sleeplessness.

Things were really going well for me. During quiet periods at the EMI office I worked on an idea I had mulled over in my mind for some years. I decided that there was an opportunity to start the score of the Irish Rhapsody I had long been planning to write for a symphony orchestra. I was able to use the office photocopier to make duplicate parts, such as those for the string section, and as soon as it was finished I copied the score and sent it to Bobby Murphy.

Eventually I had a call from the head of the symphony department at Radio Telefis Eirann to tell me that he liked the piece and to ask what its title was. I hadn't even thought of a title but off the top of my head I said 'Rhapsody in Green'. "Fine," he said. "The conductor is Colman Pearce. It will be recorded next Friday in our weekly programme and a copy tape will be sent to you in due course." I thanked him and was over the moon at the news. You can imagine my impatience waiting for the tape, which took about six weeks to arrive.

In the early 1970s something else developed that gave me new opportunities. One morning I got a phone call at the EMI office from an American bandleader and cornettist named Richard Sudhalter who was then living in London. Richard had soaked up all the characteristics of Bix Beiderbecke's playing and in fact wrote a biography of him. He told me he was planning to form a big band in the style of Paul Whiteman, with whom Bix played, and that he had the original Whiteman arrangements. He had heard I played bass sax, which would be needed to simulate the parts Adrian Rollini played with Whiteman. That was a real turn up! I was being invited to join a band of outstanding musicians and would be featured in it on the instrument I loved most.

Working with the New Paul Whiteman Orchestra for a couple of years from 1974 turned out to be one of the most satisfying phases of my professional career. Not only did we play in theatres to great acclaim, but Richard created Commodore, a small band drawn from the personnel to play in the style of Beiderbecke, Rollini and Frankie Trumbauer. The group was an immediate success. We made recordings and were given several spots on BBC Radio.

Pieces of Eight Again!

Things were certainly going well, but maybe too well. Somehow I felt a little uneasy. Sure enough, while I was in the office one day early in 1976 I had a call on the intercom from Peter Phillips, the head of EMI Music, and the son of Jimmy Phillips whom I mentioned earlier. I was wanted in Peter's office before going to lunch. The unease developed into fear as the time for my appointment with Peter approached. On my entering his lavishly carpeted office he welcomed me with a smile of portent. "Take a seat," he said, pointing to the chair opposite himself. I could see now that he was wearing the smile that says "I'm sorry, but...". "I have bad news for you," he continued, without any of the usual preamble. Straight to the point; no time to waste. "As you know, EMI policy is to give younger people an opportunity to advance in the firm and everyone who reaches the age of sixty five is automatically asked to leave. I'm afraid that includes you." In fact I was just coming up to my sixty-ninth birthday. I pointed out we had had a verbal agreement that I would stay until I reached the age of seventy. He shook his head in regret. He didn't actually say the famous words, "A verbal agreement isn't worth the paper it's written on", but his smile said it.

I asked how long I had until the job ended. "A week," he replied. I was flabbergasted. I felt the anger rising fast but I knew I had to be careful. I sat thinking for what seemed like forever. Eventually wisdom prevailed and I said, "I can see the logic but really don't you think a week is too short in my case.

Whenever we have had a hit, and needed a printed arrangement urgently, who was called at short notice to be at the printers for 8.00 a.m.? Always little me." After a brief silence he said, "OK Harry. In your case we'll make it a month," and he added, "I'll give you first refusal for any outside work that will be required." I had to be satisfied with that. But it proves that self-control pays off. I did get outside arranging, but later Peter and his brother Robin left EMI to start their own recording company. I became one of their composers, a link that eventually became profitable. One door closes and another opens!

After the end of the job at EMI, it was back to Archer Street and gigs. Then, enter trumpeter Al Wynette, who had played previously with me sometimes during the 1960s. Al was working weekends with his own band at the Café de Paris. He approached me and asked whether I would be interested in joining him. Of course I said yes. It was a good band and enjoyable to play with. Al had his own arrangements but I asked if he would like me to bring along some of my dixieland arrangements to which he agreed. The dancers were mostly good ballroom stylists. But it became immediately noticeable that the moment one of my arrangements was played they came alive. Al decided to change the routine slightly by adding a complete jive set to the normal dance tempo numbers. The policy proved a winner. Then a bombshell! One evening he told me that he had taken a job for a summer season in Yarmouth. He asked if I would lead the Café de Paris band while he was away. I agreed providing the management were happy. They were, so temporarily I became a bandleader again.

While Al was away, I led the band according to his instructions as to dance tempi, including the dixieland arrangements. When he returned he had a report from the management that was satisfactory from every point of view.

The following summer I was asked again to lead the band while Al returned to his Yarmouth gig. It was fine for me because I received extra money for leading. I learned later that I was being paid by cheque from Stan Daly whom Al had previously asked to look after the financial arrangements. Soon after Al returned from Yarmouth, however, we were told that our services would no longer be required. It seems that the Café proprietors were unhappy with the situation of Al being away.

Because the dancers had obviously liked the dixie arrangements, Bob Layzell, the clarinet player in Al's band, suggested that I ought to reform the Pieces of Eight. I wasn't really prepared to consider it at that moment. Al told me he had a Monday night gig at Alexandra Palace in north London and asked if I'd like to sit in. Since I had nothing else at the time, I agreed. It was immediately clear that the jazz was popular and Al asked me to bring in some of my arrangements. At the end of an evening's playing, he made the same suggestion as Bob Layzell that I should reform the Pieces of Eight. After the two separate propositions I decided that it might be worth having another go. Laurie, by that time, wasn't using the Pieces of Eight title. He was busy with work for EMI recordings as the main 'fixer' (booker of musicians for sessions), so there could not be a repetition of the previous fiasco.

Now it was a question of deciding on personnel. Stan Daly came in on drums and Austin Malcolm, who had a good style, became the pianist. Bob Layzell filled the clarinet chair and Al was the trumpet player. It was a stroke of luck that a great trombonist, Roy Crimmins, arrived on the scene and completed the front line of the band.[1] Al Wynette said to me

---

[1] Al Wynette played regularly with Harry for ten years from 1977. Roy Crimmins, who had worked for many years with Alex Welsh's band and with bands under his own name, played with the Pieces of Eight during the 1980s.

privately that it would be useful if I could persuade Stan Daly to act as manager because he had lots of contacts. It seems that I was a good persuader. Stan didn't hesitate and we were off! Al was right. Stan started to get us work and – guess what! – it was back to the one-night-stand touring regime.

Then an offer from America arrived. A friend named John McNally, who had lived in Farnborough but emigrated to the USA (I hadn't known where), phoned to say he was involved with a jazz society in Los Angeles. He asked if I'd like to take part in their jazz festival. I told him I would but that he would have to discuss it with my manager. I passed the inquiry to Stan Daly. I took the view that if you have a manager, he's the person to do the business. When more information came through I called a meeting of the band. It seemed that we would have to pay our own air fare but would get hotel accommodation and pay according to the number of sessions we were required to perform. Having to pay the air fare was the main obstacle.

Roy would not be able to go as he had other commitments but the rest thought it would be worth the trip if we treated it as a paid holiday. Eventually Derek Wadsworth agreed to fill the trombone slot and all was set. We arrived after a ten hour flight, completely disorientated, and were taken to the Hilton Hotel where rooms had been reserved for us. Then we discovered that we would have to pay for all food we had, including breakfast. That was where I had to intervene, as I knew John McNally very well. After some discussions it was agreed that breakfast and dinner would be provided. But that same night, around 2.00 a.m., Stan phoned my room to say that Derek's wife had died and he wanted to go back. That was

Bob Layzell began his career in the 1930s and worked with Joe Loss, Harry Roy, Lew Stone, Jock Scott among many other bands. He was with Al Wynette from 1975 and Harry Gold from the late 1970s through to the 1980s (Ed.).

a really serious problem which had to be overcome immediately.

The fact that we were able to get a flight at very short notice is nothing less than a miracle. We managed to get Derek on to a flight leaving at 6.00 a.m., but settling payment seemed as improbable a feat as our climbing Mount Everest. We knew we would have to pay but we were in California, not London. John McNally came to our rescue by guaranteeing the cheque and fortunately we found a fine local trombonist to fill Derek's place. But if ever there was a nightmare that was it, in those few hours.

We began to get back into a routine which was reasonably full but not like it had been during earlier years. And, unknown to me, fate was doing a bit of manipulation on its own behalf. We did three tours of East Germany during the mid-1980s, the period before the Berlin Wall came down. In themselves, they were more than enjoyable. The audiences were most enthusiastic and we were well looked after in a very hospitable way. But somehow, during the last tour, I had that feeling in the pit of my stomach telling me that all was not well. It turned out that I was right. On the last night of the tour there was a row between Stan and myself and I said publicly there and then that the band was now finished. Of course, after that I continued to play and I put the band together for engagements as and when the need arose. But there was no more of the incessant touring. Those years were finally over for good.

Coda

In the mid-1990s, fate took a hand again. I had been getting jazz dates at the Yorkshire Grey pub in Theobalds Road, next door to Dartmouth Chambers, where Peggy and I had our flat.

The flat was two floors up with no lift and Peggy felt that the stairs were getting too much for her. We decided we had to find another place to live. That meant taking time out to look for a flat with no stairs to climb. Eventually we found the one in which I'm now settled.

Peggy was delighted. The area is surrounded with parks and trees. Soon after we moved in, in 1995, she said, "Harry, I'd be happy to spend the rest of my life here." Her words turned out to be prophetic.

We had been out doing the weekend shopping when she complained about a pain in her chest. The doctor's surgery was closed but I had got her home and seated her in a chair when she said, "Harry, I want a doctor." I knew it was serious and phoned for an ambulance which arrived surprisingly promptly. The paramedics started to work while, unknown to me, she had stopped breathing, but they resuscitated her sufficiently to get her to hospital.

After a few weeks of steady improvement, she was advised to practise walking slowly across the ward, which she did. Then one day, while my son Morton and daughter-in-law Wendy and I were there and she was crossing the ward, she fell into my arms and passed away. I had lost the one real partner in my life and I thought it wouldn't be long before my retirement. But it was not to be.

I had lost my zest without the support of Peggy but I began to get dates for my band, which included weekends in the Duke of York pub in Clerkenwell Road. Somehow as the weeks and months went by, my attitude changed. My love for the music began to take control. The enthusiasm returned and I began to get more gigs.

At the time of writing I am 92 years of age, fit and with all my marbles, but of course without the vigour of youth. Periodically, I get a boost when I receive offers of engagements but it is obvious that they will come less frequently. As a saxophone player, I know that I can still do it and will take on anything that comes along. Have sax, will travel.

Like the footballer who is forced to hang up his boots, or the boxer to hang up his gloves, I suppose the time will come when I shall have to hang up my bass saxophone. It will need a very strong hanger to carry the weight, but I'm not yet ready. Last year (1998) I went to California, Connecticut, New York, and Cork City for the International Jazz Festival. It is a reasonable supposition that I will not yet be finally hanging up the sax, but I'm not a prophet and can't foretell the future.

One final thought. If my paternal grandfather had not changed his name to Goldberg and my father had not cut off the suffix 'berg', the Pieces of Eight could not really have existed. That's fate, isn't it?

INDEX OF NAMES

Places named are in London unless otherwise identified.